Blue Economy and the Sustainable Development Goals: Strategies for Sustainable Ocean Management and Development

I0022956

Copyright

Author: Robert C. Brears

Publisher: Global Climate Solutions

ISBNs:

eBook: 978-1-991369-39-0

Paperback: 978-1-991369-40-6

Table of Contents

Introduction

The oceans are the lifeblood of our planet, supporting ecosystems, livelihoods, and economies on a global scale. The concept of the Blue Economy offers a transformative approach to harnessing ocean resources while safeguarding their health for future generations. This chapter lays the foundation for understanding the Blue Economy and its critical role in achieving the United Nations Sustainable Development Goals (SDGs). By exploring the interconnectedness between ocean-based activities and sustainable development, it sets the stage for deeper discussions on how the Blue Economy can drive both environmental conservation and economic growth.

Definition of the Blue Economy

The Blue Economy refers to the sustainable use of ocean and coastal resources for economic growth, improved livelihoods, and the preservation of marine ecosystems. It encompasses a wide range of activities, including fisheries, aquaculture, renewable energy, maritime transport, coastal tourism, and marine biotechnology. Unlike traditional ocean-based industries, the Blue Economy is guided by principles of sustainability, equity, and resilience, ensuring that economic benefits are balanced with the long-term health of marine and coastal environments.

At its core, the Blue Economy emphasizes the integration of environmental stewardship into economic activities. It recognizes the ocean as a vital asset, not only for the resources it provides but also for the critical ecosystem services it supports, such as climate regulation, carbon sequestration, and biodiversity preservation. These services underpin the well-being of billions of people globally, particularly those in coastal and island communities.

The Blue Economy also highlights the importance of innovation and technological advancement in addressing marine challenges. Through advancements in renewable energy technologies, sustainable fisheries, and marine conservation practices, it aims to create a model of growth that is inclusive and regenerative.

Crucially, the Blue Economy aligns closely with the objectives of the United Nations SDGs, particularly SDG 14 (Life Below Water), which focuses on conserving and sustainably using the oceans, seas, and marine resources. By adopting a holistic and integrated approach, the Blue Economy provides a framework for countries, industries, and communities to balance economic development with the health of marine ecosystems, paving the way for a sustainable and equitable future. This definition serves as the foundation for exploring the potential of the Blue Economy as a driver of sustainable development in the chapters ahead.

The Role of the Oceans in Achieving Sustainable Development

The oceans are a cornerstone of life on Earth, playing a fundamental role in supporting global ecosystems, economies, and societies. Covering more than 70% of the planet's surface, they regulate the climate, provide oxygen, and serve as a critical source of food, energy, and livelihoods for billions of people. Recognizing this, the oceans are central to achieving the United Nations SDGs, particularly SDG 14, which emphasizes the need to conserve and sustainably use marine resources.

The oceans contribute directly to sustainable development in multiple ways. Fisheries and aquaculture supply nutrition and employment, particularly in developing countries, where they are vital for food security and poverty alleviation (SDG 1 and SDG 2). Coastal and marine tourism supports millions of jobs globally, providing economic benefits while fostering cultural and ecological awareness (SDG 8 and SDG 12). Additionally, the oceans offer vast potential for renewable energy generation, particularly through offshore wind, wave, and tidal energy, which are critical for advancing SDG 7 on affordable and clean energy.

Beyond these economic contributions, the oceans play a critical role in regulating the Earth's climate, acting as a carbon sink and mitigating the impacts of global warming (SDG 13). Healthy marine ecosystems also enhance biodiversity, improve water quality, and protect coastal communities from natural disasters such as storms and rising sea levels (SDG 11 and SDG 15).

However, unsustainable practices, pollution, overfishing, and climate change threaten the health of the oceans, undermining their ability to support development. Sustainable management of marine resources is essential to balance economic growth with environmental conservation, ensuring that the benefits of the oceans are preserved for future generations. By protecting and restoring ocean ecosystems, we can unlock their full potential as a driver of sustainable development.

Overview of the Sustainable Development Goals and Their Interconnections

The SDGs are a universal framework adopted by the United Nations in 2015 to address the most pressing global challenges by 2030. Comprising 17 goals and 169 targets, the SDGs aim to eradicate poverty, promote economic prosperity, ensure social equity, and protect the environment. They provide a roadmap for governments, businesses, and communities to work collectively toward a sustainable and equitable future.

At the core of the SDGs is the principle of interconnectedness, recognizing that progress in one area depends on progress in others. For example, achieving SDG 2 (Zero Hunger) requires advancements in sustainable agriculture (SDG 12), equitable water management (SDG 6), and climate resilience (SDG 13). Similarly, SDG 8 (Decent Work and Economic Growth) relies on investments in sustainable industries, inclusive education (SDG 4), and access to affordable clean energy (SDG 7).

SDG 14 (Life Below Water) is particularly critical, as healthy oceans underpin many of the other goals. Oceans contribute to food security (SDG 2), poverty reduction (SDG 1), and clean energy production (SDG 7). They also regulate the global climate, playing a vital role in achieving SDG 13 (Climate Action). However, achieving SDG 14 requires collaboration across sectors and goals, such as reducing plastic pollution (SDG 12) and strengthening international partnerships (SDG 17).

The SDGs emphasize a holistic approach to sustainable development. They acknowledge that environmental health is inseparable from economic growth and social well-being. For example, addressing inequality (SDG 10) promotes inclusive growth and fosters resilience in vulnerable communities, while sustainable urbanization (SDG 11) protects natural ecosystems and reduces carbon footprints.

The interconnected nature of the SDGs demands integrated solutions that balance competing priorities. Policies and initiatives designed to achieve one goal must account for their ripple effects on others, ensuring alignment and avoiding unintended trade-offs. This holistic perspective highlights the necessity of cross-sector collaboration and global partnerships to address complex challenges.

As a framework for action, the SDGs provide a shared vision and measurable targets to guide sustainable development. By embracing their interconnections, the global community can ensure that progress in one area accelerates progress in all, building a future that benefits people and the planet alike.

The Importance of Integrating the Blue Economy into the Global SDG Framework

The Blue Economy represents a transformative approach to balancing economic growth, environmental sustainability, and social inclusion. As the world grapples with escalating challenges such as climate change, resource depletion, and economic inequality, the

Blue Economy offers a critical pathway to achieving the SDGs. Its integration into the global SDG framework is essential to ensuring that ocean and coastal resources are utilized responsibly while addressing the interconnected goals of poverty eradication, environmental protection, and economic development.

Enhancing Economic Growth and Livelihoods

The Blue Economy plays a pivotal role in achieving SDG 1 (No Poverty) and SDG 8 (Decent Work and Economic Growth) by creating job opportunities, particularly for coastal and island communities. Fisheries, aquaculture, and maritime industries provide livelihoods for millions of people, while tourism and renewable energy sectors offer additional economic potential. Integrating the Blue Economy into the SDG framework ensures that these industries adopt sustainable practices, minimizing environmental harm while maximizing social and economic benefits.

Protecting Marine Ecosystems

Central to the Blue Economy's alignment with the SDGs is the emphasis on conserving marine ecosystems, as outlined in SDG 14 (Life Below Water). Oceans provide critical ecosystem services, such as regulating the climate, supporting biodiversity, and supplying food. However, unsustainable practices such as overfishing, pollution, and habitat destruction threaten these resources. By embedding Blue Economy principles into global efforts, it is possible to align economic activities with ecosystem conservation, achieving a balance between utilization and preservation. This also supports SDG 13 (Climate Action) by enhancing the oceans' role in carbon sequestration and climate regulation.

Fostering Innovation and Technology

The integration of the Blue Economy into the SDG framework encourages innovation and technological advancements that contribute to sustainable development. Technologies such as offshore renewable energy, sustainable aquaculture practices, and digital tools for ocean monitoring support SDG 7 (Affordable and Clean Energy) and SDG 9 (Industry, Innovation, and Infrastructure). Investing in these innovations ensures that the Blue Economy drives progress toward a greener, more sustainable global economy.

Promoting Equity and Inclusion

The Blue Economy also addresses SDG 10 (Reduced Inequalities) by focusing on equitable access to resources and opportunities. Many coastal and island communities depend on the ocean for their survival, yet they are often the most vulnerable to environmental degradation and climate change. Integrating the Blue Economy into the SDG framework ensures that these communities are included in decision-making processes and benefit from sustainable ocean-based development.

Facilitating Global Partnerships

Achieving the goals of the Blue Economy requires international collaboration, aligning with SDG 17 (Partnerships for the Goals). Oceans are a shared resource, and their sustainable management depends on cooperation among nations, industries, and organizations. Integrating Blue Economy initiatives into the SDG framework promotes coordinated action, knowledge sharing, and capacity building.

Conclusion

By integrating the Blue Economy into the global SDG framework, we can unlock its full potential as a driver of sustainable development. This approach ensures that economic growth, environmental conservation, and social equity are pursued in tandem, contributing to a resilient and inclusive future for all.

Chapter 1: Foundations of the Blue Economy

The Blue Economy represents a paradigm shift in how humanity utilizes ocean and coastal resources. This chapter explores the foundational aspects of the Blue Economy, tracing its historical evolution, defining its guiding principles, and outlining its core sectors. By examining its role in fostering sustainable development and environmental stewardship, this chapter sets the stage for understanding the transformative potential of the Blue Economy in addressing global challenges.

Historical Evolution of Ocean-Based Economies

Ocean-based economies have been integral to human civilization for thousands of years, providing sustenance, transportation, and trade opportunities. Early societies relied heavily on coastal and marine resources for survival, with fishing, shellfish gathering, and small-scale maritime trade forming the backbone of local economies. Ancient civilizations, such as those in Mesopotamia, Egypt, and the Mediterranean, utilized rivers and seas as critical conduits for commerce, connecting communities and fostering cultural exchange.

The development of advanced navigation and shipbuilding technologies marked a significant turning point in the evolution of ocean-based economies. By the 15th century, maritime exploration expanded global trade networks, ushering in an era of colonial expansion and resource exploitation. European powers established trade routes across the Atlantic, Indian, and Pacific Oceans, transporting valuable goods such as spices, textiles, and precious metals. These activities not only spurred economic growth but also laid the groundwork for modern globalization.

The Industrial Revolution in the 18th and 19th centuries further transformed ocean-based economies. Steam-powered ships revolutionized maritime transport, increasing the efficiency of goods and passenger movement. Ports became hubs of industrial activity, driving urbanization and economic development in coastal regions. The exploitation of marine resources, including fisheries, oil, and gas, intensified, contributing significantly to the economic prosperity of industrialized nations.

In the 20th century, technological advancements expanded the scope of ocean-based economies. The introduction of refrigeration and large-scale fishing fleets industrialized the fishing industry, leading to overfishing and the depletion of marine stocks. Offshore drilling became a major contributor to global energy supplies, while the emergence of coastal tourism boosted economic activity in many regions. However, these developments often came at a high environmental cost, including habitat destruction, pollution, and resource overexploitation.

The late 20th and early 21st centuries witnessed growing recognition of the environmental and social impacts of unsustainable ocean use. Global initiatives, such as the United Nations Convention on the Law of the Sea (UNCLOS) and the establishment of marine protected areas (MPAs), began to address the need for sustainable management of marine resources. The concept of the Blue Economy emerged during this time as a response to the challenges posed by traditional ocean-based economies, advocating for a balance between economic development and environmental conservation.

Today, the Blue Economy seeks to redefine the relationship between humanity and the oceans. By integrating principles of sustainability, equity, and innovation, it aims to transform ocean-based activities into drivers of inclusive and environmentally responsible growth. This shift represents the culmination of centuries of evolving ocean use, paving the way for a future where economic prosperity and marine ecosystem health are inextricably linked.

Principles of the Blue Economy: Sustainability, Equity, and Innovation

The Blue Economy is grounded in a set of guiding principles that distinguish it from traditional ocean-based economies. These principles—sustainability, equity, and innovation—form the foundation for achieving a balance between economic growth, environmental stewardship, and social inclusion. By adhering to these core values, the Blue Economy offers a transformative approach to utilizing ocean resources while ensuring their long-term viability.

Sustainability

At its core, the Blue Economy prioritizes sustainability, emphasizing the responsible use of marine and coastal resources to maintain ecological balance. Unlike conventional practices that prioritize short-term economic gains at the expense of environmental degradation, the Blue Economy seeks to ensure that economic activities do not compromise the health of marine ecosystems.

Sustainability in the Blue Economy encompasses multiple dimensions. First, it promotes the sustainable management of fisheries and aquaculture, preventing overexploitation and protecting marine biodiversity. Second, it advocates for the reduction of pollution, including plastic waste and chemical runoff, which threaten ocean health. Third, it emphasizes the importance of renewable energy, such as offshore wind, wave, and tidal energy, to reduce dependency on fossil fuels and mitigate climate change impacts.

Marine spatial planning (MSP) is a critical tool for achieving sustainability within the Blue Economy. By balancing competing demands for ocean resources—such as fishing, energy development, and tourism—this approach ensures that economic activities are conducted within the ecological limits of marine systems. This principle aligns closely with the objectives of SDG 14 (Life Below Water), which focuses on the conservation and sustainable use of oceans, seas, and marine resources.

Equity

Equity is a fundamental principle of the Blue Economy, addressing the fair distribution of benefits derived from ocean resources. This principle recognizes the disproportionate vulnerabilities faced by coastal and island communities, which often depend on the oceans for their livelihoods yet bear the brunt of environmental degradation and climate change.

The Blue Economy seeks to empower marginalized groups by ensuring equitable access to resources and opportunities. This includes providing small-scale fishers with the tools and knowledge to adopt sustainable practices, enabling their participation in global markets. It also involves prioritizing the rights of Indigenous peoples and local communities in marine governance, recognizing their traditional knowledge and stewardship of ocean resources.

Equity extends to addressing gender disparities in ocean-based industries. Women, who often play critical roles in fisheries, aquaculture, and coastal tourism, frequently face systemic barriers to equal participation and decision-making. By promoting inclusive policies and practices, the Blue Economy aims to create opportunities for all, contributing to broader social and economic development.

Moreover, the principle of equity encompasses intergenerational fairness. The Blue Economy emphasizes the need to preserve marine resources for future generations, ensuring that today's economic activities do not deplete or degrade the natural capital upon which future livelihoods depend.

Innovation

Innovation is the driving force behind the Blue Economy, enabling the development of sustainable solutions to complex challenges. By harnessing advancements in science and technology, the Blue

Economy transforms traditional industries and opens new frontiers for economic growth.

Technological innovation plays a pivotal role in optimizing resource use while minimizing environmental impacts. For example, precision aquaculture technologies use sensors and data analytics to monitor water quality and fish health, reducing waste and increasing efficiency. Similarly, innovations in renewable energy, such as floating wind turbines and wave energy converters, are unlocking the potential of marine energy while reducing greenhouse gas emissions.

Innovation in governance and policy frameworks is equally important. Adaptive management strategies, informed by real-time data and stakeholder input, allow for more effective responses to changing environmental conditions. Digital platforms and tools, such as remote sensing and satellite imagery, enhance monitoring and enforcement of marine resource use, reducing illegal activities and ensuring compliance with sustainability standards.

The Blue Economy also encourages social and business innovation. Collaborative partnerships between governments, businesses, and civil society drive the creation of innovative financial mechanisms, such as blue bonds and impact investments, to fund sustainable ocean initiatives. Public-private partnerships facilitate the scaling of solutions that benefit both the economy and the environment.

Innovation fosters resilience by equipping ocean-based industries with the tools to adapt to challenges such as climate change, resource depletion, and market volatility. It also stimulates new economic opportunities, from marine biotechnology to eco-tourism, creating pathways for sustainable growth.

By combining sustainability, equity, and innovation, the Blue Economy offers a holistic and forward-thinking framework for ocean-based development. These principles ensure that economic activities align with the preservation of marine ecosystems, the empowerment of communities, and the pursuit of technological and social progress. Through this approach, the Blue Economy paves the way for a more sustainable and inclusive future.

Key Components: Fisheries, Aquaculture, Shipping, Tourism, Renewable Energy, and Marine Biotechnology

The Blue Economy encompasses a diverse range of sectors that collectively contribute to sustainable ocean-based economic growth. These components—fisheries, aquaculture, shipping, tourism, renewable energy, and marine biotechnology—play pivotal roles in driving economic activity while addressing environmental and social challenges. By integrating sustainability and innovation into these industries, the Blue Economy transforms traditional practices and unlocks new opportunities for development.

Fisheries

Fisheries are a cornerstone of the Blue Economy, providing a critical source of food, income, and employment for millions worldwide. Small-scale and industrial fishing sectors contribute significantly to food security, especially in coastal and developing nations. However, overfishing and destructive practices have led to the depletion of fish stocks, threatening marine biodiversity and the livelihoods of fishing communities.

Sustainable fisheries management is essential for aligning the sector with the principles of the Blue Economy. Measures such as setting catch limits, protecting spawning areas, and reducing bycatch ensure the long-term health of fish populations. Technological advancements, including satellite monitoring and data-driven stock assessments, enable more effective regulation and enforcement of sustainable practices. By adopting these approaches, fisheries can continue to support economic growth while conserving marine ecosystems.

Aquaculture

Aquaculture, or the farming of aquatic organisms, is the fastest-growing food production sector globally. It provides a sustainable alternative to wild fisheries, reducing pressure on natural fish stocks while meeting the rising demand for seafood. Key species cultivated include finfish, shellfish, and seaweed, which serve as important sources of protein, nutrients, and bio-based products.

Sustainable aquaculture practices are critical to minimizing environmental impacts such as habitat degradation, water pollution, and disease outbreaks. Innovations like integrated multi-trophic aquaculture (IMTA), which combines different species in a single system to enhance resource efficiency, demonstrate how the sector can align with the Blue Economy's goals. Additionally, aquaculture can contribute to climate resilience by providing livelihoods for coastal communities affected by declining wild fish stocks.

Shipping

Shipping is the backbone of global trade, responsible for transporting more than 80% of the world's goods. While it is a vital component of the Blue Economy, the shipping industry faces significant challenges related to greenhouse gas emissions, marine pollution, and habitat destruction caused by shipping routes and port operations.

Decarbonizing the shipping sector is a key priority for integrating it into the Blue Economy. Transitioning to low-carbon fuels, such as liquefied natural gas (LNG), hydrogen, and ammonia, can significantly reduce emissions. The adoption of energy-efficient ship designs, digital technologies for route optimization, and stricter regulations on ballast water management further enhance environmental sustainability. Additionally, investments in green ports—equipped with renewable energy infrastructure and waste management systems—can mitigate the sector's ecological footprint.

Tourism

Coastal and marine tourism is a major economic driver, generating significant revenue and employment opportunities for many nations. From beach resorts to marine parks, this sector attracts millions of visitors annually, offering unique experiences tied to natural and cultural heritage. However, unsustainable tourism practices, including habitat destruction, overdevelopment, and pollution, pose serious threats to marine ecosystems.

The Blue Economy promotes sustainable tourism models that balance economic benefits with environmental conservation. Eco-tourism, for example, focuses on low-impact activities that educate visitors about marine ecosystems while supporting local communities. Certification schemes, such as the Blue Flag program, encourage tourism operators to adopt sustainable practices, including waste management, energy efficiency, and biodiversity protection. By prioritizing sustainability, tourism can remain a vibrant and resilient component of the Blue Economy.

Renewable Energy

The oceans hold immense potential for renewable energy production, making the sector a critical pillar of the Blue Economy. Technologies such as offshore wind turbines, wave energy converters, and tidal energy systems harness oceanic resources to generate clean, reliable power. These innovations contribute to reducing global dependence on fossil fuels, aligning with the objectives of SDG 7 (Affordable and Clean Energy) and SDG 13 (Climate Action).

Offshore renewable energy offers additional benefits beyond power generation. It creates employment opportunities, enhances energy security, and supports the electrification of remote coastal and island communities. However, the development of renewable energy infrastructure must consider potential environmental impacts, such as habitat disruption and risks to marine species. Strategic site selection, stakeholder engagement, and advances in technology help mitigate these challenges while maximizing the sector's potential.

Marine Biotechnology

Marine biotechnology represents a rapidly emerging field with transformative implications for the Blue Economy. It involves the exploration and utilization of marine organisms and ecosystems for a wide range of applications, from medicine to biofuels. Marine-derived compounds have already yielded breakthroughs in pharmaceuticals, including antibiotics and cancer treatments, while seaweed and algae are being used to produce sustainable materials and alternative energy sources.

The potential of marine biotechnology extends to environmental restoration. Bioremediation techniques, which use marine organisms to clean up pollutants, offer solutions for addressing issues like oil spills and plastic waste. Additionally, innovations in biomaterials, such as biodegradable plastics made from marine algae, contribute to reducing the environmental footprint of various industries.

Sustainability is integral to the development of marine biotechnology. Responsible exploration of marine biodiversity and adherence to ethical and regulatory standards ensure that this field aligns with the principles of the Blue Economy. By fostering innovation, marine biotechnology not only drives economic growth but also supports environmental resilience and human well-being.

Each of these components contributes uniquely to the Blue Economy, offering pathways to sustainable development while addressing key global challenges. By integrating sustainability, equity, and innovation into these sectors, the Blue Economy transforms traditional ocean-based industries into drivers of long-term economic and ecological prosperity.

The Blue Economy as a Driver of Economic Growth and Environmental Conservation

The Blue Economy represents a transformative approach to ocean-based industries, demonstrating that economic growth and environmental conservation can coexist. By prioritizing sustainable practices, innovation, and equitable resource use, the Blue Economy addresses global challenges while unlocking opportunities for long-term prosperity.

One of the primary ways the Blue Economy drives economic growth is by creating diverse revenue streams. Industries such as fisheries, aquaculture, coastal tourism, renewable energy, and marine biotechnology generate significant employment and income, particularly in coastal and island communities. Sustainable fisheries and aquaculture support food security and livelihoods, while renewable energy technologies, such as offshore wind and tidal energy, contribute to energy security and green job creation. Coastal tourism remains a cornerstone of economic activity, drawing millions of visitors annually, while marine biotechnology opens new frontiers for high-value products in medicine, energy, and materials.

In addition to supporting economic growth, the Blue Economy emphasizes environmental conservation as a cornerstone of its framework. Sustainable practices across industries minimize negative impacts on marine ecosystems, ensuring the health of oceans for future generations. MSP and ecosystem-based management approaches help balance competing interests, such as fishing, tourism, and energy development, while protecting critical habitats and biodiversity. For instance, MPAs not only preserve ecosystems but also enhance fish stocks, leading to more stable and sustainable fisheries.

Innovation plays a central role in aligning economic growth with environmental conservation. Advances in technology, such as precision aquaculture, digital monitoring of marine ecosystems, and eco-friendly ship designs, enable industries to optimize resource use while reducing pollution and waste. Financial mechanisms, such as blue bonds and impact investing, further incentivize sustainable development by channeling funds into projects that benefit both the economy and the environment.

By integrating economic and environmental objectives, the Blue Economy offers a model for inclusive and sustainable growth. It provides a pathway for countries to leverage their marine resources responsibly, fostering resilience, equity, and prosperity while protecting the health of the planet's oceans.

Chapter 2: The Blue Economy's Contribution to the SDGs

The Blue Economy is uniquely positioned to advance the United Nations SDGs by aligning ocean-based economic activities with environmental sustainability and social equity. This chapter explores how the Blue Economy contributes to specific SDGs, including those related to poverty eradication, climate action, and biodiversity conservation, while emphasizing its role as a cross-cutting enabler of global sustainable development.

Synergies Between the Blue Economy and Individual SDGs

The Blue Economy holds the potential to drive transformative change across multiple sectors, aligning closely with the United Nations SDGs. As ocean-based industries continue to grow, their role in achieving sustainable development becomes increasingly important. By promoting the sustainable use of marine resources, the Blue Economy directly supports key SDGs, including those focused on poverty reduction, climate action, and life below water. However, the connections between the Blue Economy and these global goals are not one-dimensional; they create powerful synergies that foster environmental sustainability, economic growth, and social inclusion. This section explores how the Blue Economy intersects with individual SDGs, highlighting the mutual benefits and reinforcing the importance of integrated approaches for sustainable development.

SDG 14 (Life Below Water): Central to the Blue Economy

Sustainable Development Goal 14 (Life Below Water) is at the heart of the Blue Economy, focusing on the conservation and sustainable use of oceans, seas, and marine resources. Oceans cover more than 70% of the Earth's surface and play a vital role in supporting life, regulating the climate, and driving economic activities. The Blue Economy directly aligns with SDG 14's targets by promoting practices that ensure the health and productivity of marine ecosystems while enabling economic growth.

The targets of SDG 14 address critical challenges such as marine pollution, overfishing, habitat destruction, and ocean acidification. Tackling marine pollution, for instance, is essential for maintaining clean and productive oceans. The Blue Economy incorporates measures to reduce waste and improve waste management, particularly in sectors like shipping and tourism. Innovations such as biodegradable materials and circular economy practices are key to achieving this goal, ensuring that economic activities do not compromise marine health.

Sustainable Fisheries and Aquaculture

Sustainable fisheries and aquaculture are also integral to SDG 14 and the Blue Economy. Overfishing threatens global fish stocks, undermining food security and livelihoods, especially in developing countries. The Blue Economy emphasizes science-based management practices, such as setting catch limits and protecting breeding grounds, to restore and maintain fish populations. Sustainable aquaculture provides an alternative to wild capture fisheries, reducing pressure on natural stocks while meeting growing global demand for seafood.

Protecting marine biodiversity is another cornerstone of SDG 14. Marine ecosystems, such as coral reefs, mangroves, and seagrass beds, provide critical habitats for countless species while delivering ecosystem services like carbon sequestration and coastal protection. The Blue Economy supports the establishment and management of MPAs to conserve biodiversity. These areas not only safeguard ecosystems but also enhance the resilience of ocean-based industries by preserving the natural resources upon which they depend.

Climate Change Mitigation and Adaptation

Climate change mitigation and adaptation are closely tied to SDG 14. Oceans act as a carbon sink, absorbing significant amounts of greenhouse gases, but rising temperatures and acidification pose severe threats to marine life. The Blue Economy promotes renewable energy solutions, such as offshore wind and tidal energy, that reduce carbon emissions while minimizing impacts on marine ecosystems. Additionally, nature-based solutions, such as restoring mangroves and seagrasses, help coastal communities adapt to climate change by protecting against storm surges and erosion.

Collaboration and partnerships are essential to achieving SDG 14, aligning with the Blue Economy's emphasis on multi-stakeholder engagement. Governments, businesses, and civil society must work together to implement policies, invest in sustainable practices, and build capacity for ocean conservation. Initiatives such as MSP and international agreements like the UNCLOS provide frameworks for balancing economic activities with ecosystem preservation.

Through its alignment with SDG 14, the Blue Economy highlights the interconnectedness of ocean health and human well-being. By fostering sustainable practices across sectors, it ensures that the oceans remain a vital resource for future generations while supporting global economic and environmental goals.

SDG 1 (No Poverty) and SDG 8 (Decent Work and Economic Growth): Coastal Livelihoods

The Blue Economy plays a pivotal role in addressing SDG 1 (No Poverty) and SDG 8 (Decent Work and Economic Growth) by fostering sustainable livelihoods and driving economic development in coastal and marine regions. Oceans and coastal areas provide essential resources and opportunities for millions of people, particularly in developing nations, where coastal communities often depend on marine resources for survival and income. Integrating Blue Economy principles into these activities ensures the sustainable use of resources while creating long-term economic benefits.

Coastal Livelihoods and Poverty Reduction

Coastal communities are among the most vulnerable to poverty due to limited access to resources, economic opportunities, and infrastructure. Fisheries, aquaculture, and small-scale maritime activities are lifelines for these communities, providing food security and income for millions of households worldwide. However, unsustainable practices, overfishing, and climate change threaten these resources, exacerbating poverty and inequality.

The Blue Economy addresses these challenges by promoting sustainable management of marine resources. For example, empowering small-scale fishers with access to better technologies, training, and markets enhances their productivity and income while reducing pressure on fish stocks. Diversification of livelihoods, such as engaging in sustainable aquaculture or eco-tourism, further reduces economic dependency on a single resource, building resilience against environmental and economic shocks.

Infrastructure development also plays a critical role in poverty reduction. Investments in ports, markets, and cold storage facilities enable coastal communities to participate more effectively in local and global markets. These developments not only increase income opportunities but also improve access to essential services, such as education and healthcare, breaking the cycle of poverty.

Decent Work and Economic Growth in Coastal Regions

The Blue Economy is a significant driver of economic growth, contributing to GDP and employment in many countries. Industries such as fishing, aquaculture, tourism, and shipping create millions of jobs globally, particularly in coastal and island regions. However, ensuring decent work within these industries requires addressing issues such as low wages, unsafe working conditions, and exploitation of vulnerable populations.

By emphasizing equity and sustainability, the Blue Economy seeks to create jobs that uphold labor rights and provide fair wages. For instance, transitioning fisheries to sustainable practices often leads to more stable and predictable incomes for workers by ensuring the long-term availability of marine resources. Similarly, fostering sustainable tourism initiatives generates jobs in hospitality, transportation, and conservation, offering diverse opportunities for local populations.

Renewable energy projects in coastal areas also contribute to job creation. Offshore wind farms, wave energy installations, and other clean energy projects require skilled labor for construction, operation, and maintenance. These projects not only provide employment but also contribute to the global transition toward a low-carbon economy, aligning with SDG 13 (Climate Action) while supporting SDG 8.

Empowering Women and Marginalized Groups

The Blue Economy addresses systemic inequities in coastal livelihoods by empowering women and marginalized groups. Women often play critical roles in marine industries, such as processing and marketing seafood, yet they frequently face barriers to fair pay, leadership, and decision-making opportunities. By promoting inclusive policies and capacity-building initiatives, the Blue Economy enables greater participation and economic independence for women in coastal communities.

Supporting marginalized groups also involves recognizing the rights and contributions of Indigenous peoples and local communities. Many of these groups have traditional knowledge and sustainable practices that can enhance the resilience of ocean-based industries. Ensuring their inclusion in resource management and economic activities is essential for creating equitable and sustainable coastal livelihoods.

Building Resilience Through Sustainable Practices

Resilience is a key component of reducing poverty and fostering economic growth in coastal regions. Climate change, overexploitation of resources, and natural disasters disproportionately affect coastal communities. The Blue Economy mitigates these risks by encouraging sustainable practices, such as mangrove restoration, which protects coastlines from erosion while supporting fisheries and biodiversity. MSP further ensures that economic activities do not conflict with environmental conservation, preserving resources for future generations.

Through its focus on sustainability, equity, and innovation, the Blue Economy supports SDG 1 and SDG 8 by creating resilient and inclusive economic opportunities for coastal communities. By fostering sustainable livelihoods and ensuring decent work, it addresses poverty while driving economic growth, ensuring that no one is left behind.

SDG 13 (Climate Action): Ocean-Based Climate Mitigation and Adaptation Strategies

The Blue Economy plays a crucial role in advancing SDG 13 (Climate Action) by leveraging ocean-based solutions for climate mitigation and adaptation. Oceans are integral to regulating the global climate, acting as a carbon sink and buffering against the impacts of climate change. However, rising temperatures, ocean acidification, and sea level rise threaten marine ecosystems and the livelihoods dependent on them. Through sustainable practices and innovative technologies, the Blue Economy offers pathways to address these challenges while contributing to global climate goals.

Ocean-Based Mitigation Strategies

Oceans are one of the planet's largest carbon sinks, absorbing nearly a quarter of all carbon dioxide emissions. Preserving and enhancing this capacity is essential for mitigating climate change. The Blue Economy promotes strategies that protect and restore marine ecosystems, such as mangroves, seagrasses, and salt marshes, which are known as "blue carbon" ecosystems. These habitats sequester large amounts of carbon while also supporting biodiversity and coastal protection.

Marine renewable energy is another key component of ocean-based mitigation. Offshore wind, wave, and tidal energy offer significant potential for reducing reliance on fossil fuels. By generating clean energy, these technologies contribute to global decarbonization efforts and reduce greenhouse gas emissions. Advances in floating wind turbines and wave energy converters are expanding the reach of these solutions, making them viable even in deeper waters.

The shipping industry, a major contributor to global emissions, is also transitioning toward sustainability within the Blue Economy framework. Decarbonization efforts include the adoption of low-carbon fuels, such as hydrogen and ammonia, and the use of energy-efficient ship designs. Digital technologies, such as route optimization and emissions monitoring, further enhance the sector's capacity to reduce its carbon footprint.

Ocean-Based Adaptation Strategies

Adaptation to the impacts of climate change is equally important, particularly for coastal communities that face heightened risks from rising sea levels, storm surges, and extreme weather events. The Blue Economy prioritizes nature-based solutions, which provide cost-effective and resilient defenses against these challenges. For example, restoring mangroves and coral reefs not only sequesters carbon but also reduces wave energy, protecting coastal infrastructure and communities from erosion and flooding.

MSP is another critical tool for climate adaptation. By integrating climate risk assessments into spatial planning processes, MSP ensures that economic activities, such as fisheries and tourism, do not exacerbate vulnerabilities to climate impacts. It also helps allocate space for renewable energy projects and conservation zones, balancing development with resilience.

Aquaculture, particularly seaweed farming, contributes to both mitigation and adaptation. Seaweed absorbs carbon and nutrients, reducing ocean acidification locally while providing sustainable food and biofuel sources. Coastal aquaculture systems can also be designed to withstand climate impacts, offering stable livelihoods even in the face of environmental changes.

Research and Innovation for Climate Action

Innovation and scientific research are at the forefront of ocean-based climate action. Advancements in marine monitoring technologies, such as satellite imagery and autonomous underwater vehicles, improve our ability to track climate impacts and develop targeted responses. These tools enable more effective management of marine ecosystems, ensuring their resilience and continued role in climate mitigation.

Emerging solutions, such as ocean-based carbon capture and storage (CCS), are gaining attention as a potential means to remove carbon from the atmosphere. While still in development, these technologies could complement natural carbon sinks, offering an additional tool in the fight against climate change. The Blue Economy provides a platform for scaling such innovations, ensuring their integration into broader climate strategies.

Empowering Communities Through Climate Solutions

The Blue Economy also emphasizes the importance of empowering coastal and island communities to participate in climate action. Capacity-building programs, financial support, and inclusive governance ensure that these communities can implement adaptation measures and benefit from emerging opportunities in renewable energy and sustainable aquaculture. By prioritizing local involvement, the Blue Economy aligns with the principle of equity, ensuring that vulnerable populations are not left behind in the transition to a climate-resilient future.

Through its focus on mitigation, adaptation, and innovation, the Blue Economy aligns ocean-based activities with global climate goals, demonstrating that sustainable use of marine resources can simultaneously address environmental, economic, and social challenges.

Blue Economy as a Cross-Cutting Enabler of Multiple SDGs

The Blue Economy is uniquely positioned as a cross-cutting enabler of the United Nations SDGs, driving progress on economic, environmental, and social fronts. By integrating sustainability into ocean-based activities, it bridges the gaps between individual SDGs, fostering synergies that amplify their collective impact. Through its interconnected nature, the Blue Economy supports a holistic approach to addressing global challenges, from poverty eradication and climate resilience to biodiversity conservation and inclusive development.

Economic Growth and Poverty Alleviation (SDGs 1 and 8)

The Blue Economy significantly contributes to reducing poverty (SDG 1) and promoting decent work and economic growth (SDG 8). Coastal and marine sectors, such as fisheries, aquaculture, tourism, and renewable energy, provide livelihoods for millions, particularly in developing countries. Small-scale fisheries, for example, are vital for food security and income generation in coastal communities. Sustainable aquaculture further enhances these benefits by reducing overfishing while creating stable job opportunities.

The Blue Economy also supports inclusive economic growth by diversifying income streams. Industries like marine biotechnology and eco-tourism offer high-value, sustainable alternatives to traditional extractive activities. By fostering innovation and providing access to global markets, the Blue Economy ensures that economic opportunities are distributed equitably, reducing inequalities and empowering marginalized communities.

Climate Action and Resilience (SDGs 13 and 11)

As the world grapples with the impacts of climate change, the Blue Economy plays a pivotal role in advancing SDG 13 (Climate Action) and SDG 11 (Sustainable Cities and Communities). Oceans act as natural climate regulators, absorbing carbon dioxide and buffering against extreme weather events. Protecting and restoring marine ecosystems, such as mangroves, seagrasses, and coral reefs, enhances their capacity to mitigate climate impacts while safeguarding coastal communities from storm surges and erosion.

The Blue Economy also drives the transition to renewable energy, with offshore wind, wave, and tidal energy providing clean, reliable power. These innovations not only contribute to reducing greenhouse gas emissions but also create jobs and strengthen energy security, aligning with broader sustainability goals. Additionally, MSP integrates climate risk assessments, ensuring that economic activities enhance rather than undermine climate resilience.

Environmental Sustainability and Biodiversity (SDGs 14 and 15)

The Blue Economy directly supports SDG 14 (Life Below Water) and SDG 15 (Life on Land) by prioritizing the conservation and sustainable use of marine and coastal ecosystems. Marine biodiversity is essential for maintaining ecological balance, supporting food chains, and providing ecosystem services such as carbon sequestration and water purification. The establishment of MPAs and the adoption of sustainable practices in industries like fisheries and tourism ensure the long-term health of these ecosystems.

The Blue Economy also addresses land-based environmental challenges that impact marine environments, such as pollution and deforestation. By promoting circular economy principles and reducing plastic waste, it mitigates the flow of pollutants into the oceans. Furthermore, integrating nature-based solutions, such as wetland restoration, enhances biodiversity and strengthens the resilience of interconnected land and sea ecosystems.

Innovation, Infrastructure, and Technology (SDGs 9 and 7)

Innovation and infrastructure development are central to the Blue Economy's ability to drive progress across multiple SDGs. Advanced technologies, such as satellite monitoring, data analytics, and autonomous vehicles, improve the management of marine resources and enable more efficient, sustainable operations across industries. For instance, precision aquaculture technologies optimize resource use while minimizing environmental impacts, supporting both SDG 9 (Industry, Innovation, and Infrastructure) and SDG 7 (Affordable and Clean Energy).

Infrastructure investments, such as green ports and renewable energy installations, further align with the Blue Economy's objectives. These projects reduce the environmental footprint of shipping and energy production while creating jobs and facilitating economic development. Innovations in marine biotechnology also contribute to SDG 9 by unlocking new possibilities for pharmaceuticals, biofuels, and sustainable materials.

Social Equity and Inclusive Development (SDGs 10 and 5)

The Blue Economy emphasizes social equity, aligning with SDG 10 (Reduced Inequalities) and SDG 5 (Gender Equality). Coastal and island communities, often among the most vulnerable to environmental degradation and economic marginalization, benefit directly from the Blue Economy's focus on equitable resource distribution and inclusive governance. Capacity-building initiatives and access to sustainable income opportunities empower these communities, ensuring their active participation in decision-making processes.

Gender equality is also a priority within the Blue Economy framework. Women play vital roles in sectors such as fisheries, aquaculture, and coastal tourism, yet they often face systemic barriers to fair pay, leadership, and access to resources. By promoting inclusive policies and removing structural obstacles, the Blue Economy ensures that women have equal opportunities to contribute to and benefit from sustainable ocean-based development.

Partnerships and Global Collaboration (SDG 17)

Achieving the full potential of the Blue Economy requires robust partnerships and international collaboration, aligning with SDG 17 (Partnerships for the Goals). Oceans are a shared resource, and their sustainable management depends on coordinated efforts across nations, industries, and organizations. Initiatives such as the UNCLOS, MSP, and blue finance mechanisms demonstrate the importance of collective action in addressing complex challenges.

Public-private partnerships are particularly effective in mobilizing resources and scaling innovative solutions. For example, blue bonds and impact investments channel funds into projects that benefit both the economy and the environment, fostering a global shift toward sustainability. Knowledge-sharing platforms and capacity-building programs further enhance collaboration, ensuring that best practices are adopted and adapted worldwide.

By integrating economic, environmental, and social priorities, the Blue Economy acts as a cross-cutting enabler of multiple SDGs. Its holistic approach demonstrates the interconnectedness of sustainable development goals, highlighting the importance of leveraging synergies to create a future that is equitable, resilient, and environmentally sustainable.

Chapter 3: Governance and Policy Frameworks for the Blue Economy

Effective governance and robust policy frameworks are essential to unlocking the full potential of the Blue Economy while ensuring sustainability and equity. This chapter examines the international agreements, national strategies, and regulatory tools that guide the sustainable use of marine resources. It also explores the challenges of policy coordination and the need for innovative approaches to balance economic growth with environmental conservation.

International Agreements and Initiatives: UNCLOS, CBD, and SDG 14 Targets

The sustainable management of ocean resources relies heavily on international agreements and initiatives that provide a legal and institutional framework for the Blue Economy. Key agreements such as the UNCLOS, the Convention on Biological Diversity (CBD), and the targets set under Sustainable Development Goal 14 (SDG 14) guide global efforts to balance economic activities with the conservation of marine ecosystems. These frameworks foster cooperation, establish norms, and provide mechanisms to address the complex and transboundary nature of marine resource management.

UNCLOS

Adopted in 1982, UNCLOS is often referred to as the "Constitution of the Oceans." It provides a comprehensive legal framework governing the use of the world's seas and oceans, addressing issues such as maritime boundaries, navigation rights, and the exploitation of marine resources. UNCLOS establishes principles for the sustainable management of ocean resources while balancing the interests of coastal states, landlocked nations, and the global community.

One of the key contributions of UNCLOS to the Blue Economy is its focus on Exclusive Economic Zones (EEZs). Coastal states have sovereign rights to explore and exploit resources within 200 nautical miles of their shores, enabling them to harness the economic potential of their marine environments. However, UNCLOS also imposes obligations to conserve and sustainably manage these resources, aligning with the principles of the Blue Economy.

UNCLOS also plays a critical role in addressing environmental challenges, such as marine pollution and overfishing. It requires states to take measures to prevent, reduce, and control pollution from land-based and maritime sources, ensuring that economic activities do not compromise the health of marine ecosystems. Furthermore, it promotes cooperation in scientific research, capacity building, and technology transfer, fostering innovation and equitable access to ocean resources.

CBD

The Convention on Biological Diversity, adopted in 1992, is a global treaty aimed at conserving biodiversity, ensuring sustainable use of natural resources, and promoting the fair and equitable sharing of benefits arising from their use. Marine and coastal biodiversity is a significant focus of the CBD, as healthy ecosystems are essential for the sustainability of the Blue Economy.

Through initiatives such as the Aichi Biodiversity Targets and the post-2020 Global Biodiversity Framework, the CBD establishes goals and action plans to protect marine ecosystems. Key targets include expanding MPAs, restoring degraded habitats, and reducing pressures on biodiversity caused by overfishing, pollution, and climate change. These efforts align with the Blue Economy's emphasis on balancing economic development with ecological integrity.

The CBD also encourages the integration of biodiversity considerations into marine governance. For example, ecosystem-based approaches to fisheries management ensure that economic activities do not undermine the ecological balance of marine environments. By fostering partnerships between governments, businesses, and communities, the CBD creates a platform for collaborative action that supports both biodiversity conservation and sustainable economic growth.

Sustainable Development Goal 14 (SDG 14) Targets

SDG 14, part of the United Nations' 2030 Agenda for Sustainable Development, is dedicated to "Life Below Water." Its targets address critical challenges facing the oceans, including overfishing, pollution, habitat destruction, and climate change. As a cornerstone of the Blue Economy, SDG 14 provides a roadmap for integrating sustainable practices into ocean-based industries while ensuring the long-term health of marine ecosystems.

The SDG 14 targets are diverse and ambitious, covering a range of issues vital to the Blue Economy. These include:

• **Reducing marine pollution (Target 14.1):** Promoting waste reduction and improving waste management systems to minimize the impact of plastics and other pollutants on marine ecosystems.

• **Sustainable management of fisheries (Target 14.4):** Ending overfishing, illegal, unreported, and unregulated (IUU) fishing, and destructive fishing practices to restore fish stocks.

• **Protecting marine biodiversity (Target 14.5):** Expanding MPAs to cover at least 10% of coastal and marine areas, safeguarding critical habitats and species.

• **Enhancing the economic benefits of sustainable ocean use (Target 14.7):** Supporting small island developing states (SIDS) and least developed countries (LDCs) in harnessing the potential of the Blue Economy for sustainable growth.

SDG 14 emphasizes the interconnectedness of environmental health and economic prosperity. By aligning national policies and international collaborations with these targets, the Blue Economy contributes to achieving broader sustainable development objectives.

Synergies Between Agreements and Initiatives

The UNCLOS, CBD, and SDG 14 targets are complementary, reinforcing the principles of sustainability, equity, and innovation that underpin the Blue Economy. UNCLOS provides a legal foundation for resource use, the CBD ensures the integration of biodiversity considerations, and SDG 14 establishes actionable goals for ocean conservation. Together, these frameworks create a cohesive system for addressing the complex challenges of managing marine resources in a sustainable and inclusive manner.

By adhering to these agreements and initiatives, countries can align their Blue Economy strategies with global standards, fostering cooperation and shared accountability. This approach ensures that economic activities in the marine environment contribute not only to national development but also to the preservation of global ecological and social systems.

National and Regional Blue Economy Strategies

National and regional Blue Economy strategies are essential for translating global commitments into localized action. These strategies provide tailored frameworks that align economic development with sustainability and equity, enabling countries and regions to harness their unique marine resources responsibly. By integrating the principles of the Blue Economy into governance, policies, and development plans, nations can address specific challenges while maximizing opportunities for economic growth, environmental protection, and social inclusion.

National Blue Economy Strategies

At the national level, Blue Economy strategies are designed to align with a country's specific geographic, economic, and environmental contexts. Coastal and island nations often lead in developing these strategies, recognizing the vast potential of their marine resources to drive sustainable development. National strategies typically focus on key sectors such as fisheries, aquaculture, tourism, renewable energy, and shipping, while addressing cross-cutting issues like climate change, biodiversity loss, and pollution.

For example, SIDs often prioritize tourism and fisheries as economic pillars while incorporating renewable energy and ecosystem conservation into their Blue Economy frameworks. By diversifying economic activities, these nations reduce dependency on a single resource, increasing resilience to global economic fluctuations and environmental challenges.

National strategies also emphasize the role of governance in ensuring sustainable outcomes. This includes strengthening institutions, enhancing capacity for resource management, and implementing policies to regulate industries. For instance, countries often adopt sustainable fisheries management practices, such as setting quotas, enforcing anti-illegal fishing measures, and promoting science-based decision-making. Similarly, investments in renewable energy, such as offshore wind or tidal power, are incorporated into national plans to achieve energy security while reducing greenhouse gas emissions.

Regional Blue Economy Strategies

At the regional level, Blue Economy strategies foster cooperation among neighboring countries that share marine ecosystems and resources. Collaborative approaches are particularly important in addressing transboundary challenges, such as overfishing, pollution, and maritime security. Regional strategies align with international agreements while addressing the specific needs and priorities of the region.

In Africa, for example, the African Union's Blue Economy Strategy focuses on sustainable resource use, maritime safety, and regional integration. By coordinating efforts across member states, the strategy aims to unlock the potential of Africa's vast coastline and EEZs, contributing to economic diversification, food security, and environmental conservation.

Similarly, in the Pacific, regional Blue Economy initiatives focus on the shared challenges faced by small island nations, such as rising sea levels, climate impacts, and overexploitation of fisheries. Regional organizations, such as the Pacific Islands Forum, promote collective action through resource-sharing agreements, capacity-building programs, and joint MSP efforts.

The European Union (EU) also plays a leading role in regional Blue Economy governance, particularly through its Integrated Maritime Policy and the European Green Deal. These initiatives promote sustainable growth in maritime sectors, including offshore renewable energy, sustainable aquaculture, and marine biodiversity conservation. The EU's regional strategies emphasize innovation, data sharing, and public-private partnerships to enhance the efficiency and sustainability of marine resource use.

Common Elements of Successful Strategies

While national and regional Blue Economy strategies vary in scope and focus, successful frameworks often share common elements:

1. **Stakeholder Engagement:** Effective strategies involve collaboration among governments, businesses, local communities, and civil society to ensure inclusive and equitable decision-making.

2. **Marine Spatial Planning:** Integrating MSP into strategies helps balance competing demands for ocean space while minimizing environmental impacts.

3. **Data-Driven Decision-Making:** Access to reliable scientific data and technological tools enhances resource management and policy development.

4. **Capacity Building and Education:** Training and knowledge-sharing programs empower communities and institutions to implement sustainable practices.

5. **Sustainable Financing:** Strategies often include mechanisms such as blue bonds and public-private partnerships to mobilize funding for sustainable initiatives.

Challenges in Implementation

Despite their benefits, national and regional Blue Economy strategies face challenges in implementation. Limited financial resources, weak governance structures, and lack of capacity can hinder progress, particularly in developing nations. Additionally, balancing economic growth with environmental conservation requires careful planning and coordination among stakeholders. Ensuring alignment with global frameworks, such as the SDGs, adds another layer of complexity.

By addressing these challenges through targeted interventions and collaborative efforts, national and regional Blue Economy strategies can unlock the potential of marine resources while safeguarding the health of oceans for future generations. Through localized approaches that reflect global principles, they provide a foundation for sustainable development and resilience in the face of environmental and economic uncertainties.

Integrating the Blue Economy into National Development Plans

Integrating the Blue Economy into national development plans is critical for unlocking the economic and environmental potential of marine and coastal resources. By embedding the principles of sustainability, equity, and innovation into broader development strategies, countries can align economic growth with environmental conservation and social well-being. This approach ensures that the Blue Economy contributes to long-term national objectives while addressing global challenges such as climate change, biodiversity loss, and poverty.

Economic Prioritization of Marine Sectors

National development plans that include the Blue Economy prioritize key marine sectors such as fisheries, aquaculture, renewable energy, coastal tourism, and shipping. These sectors serve as engines of economic growth, generating employment, income, and foreign exchange. By strategically integrating these sectors into development plans, governments can create synergies with other areas, such as infrastructure development, industrial growth, and trade.

For instance, the promotion of offshore renewable energy not only addresses energy security but also stimulates innovation and investment in technology. Similarly, sustainable aquaculture contributes to food security while reducing the strain on wild fish stocks. When marine and coastal activities are recognized as central to economic planning, their contributions to GDP and employment become more predictable and resilient.

Environmental Sustainability and Ecosystem Protection

The integration of the Blue Economy into development plans emphasizes the protection and restoration of marine ecosystems, which are vital for sustaining economic activities and ensuring ecological balance. MSP and ecosystem-based management are key tools used to incorporate sustainability into national strategies. These approaches help allocate ocean space for various uses, such as fishing, tourism, and conservation, while minimizing conflicts and environmental degradation.

Additionally, development plans that integrate the Blue Economy often include policies to combat marine pollution, promote circular economy principles, and mitigate the impacts of climate change. For example, initiatives to reduce plastic waste and improve waste management systems align marine conservation efforts with broader environmental goals, supporting both economic and ecological sustainability.

Social Inclusion and Equity

Integrating the Blue Economy into national plans also requires a focus on social inclusion and equity. Coastal communities, which are often marginalized and vulnerable to environmental and economic shocks, must be actively involved in decision-making processes. Ensuring equitable access to marine resources, income opportunities, and capacity-building programs is essential for reducing inequalities and fostering resilience.

Development plans often address this by incorporating specific measures to empower small-scale fishers, women, and Indigenous peoples who depend on marine resources. Training programs, microfinance initiatives, and market access schemes enable these groups to participate in and benefit from Blue Economy activities. By addressing social equity, national plans create inclusive pathways for sustainable development.

Policy and Governance Integration

Effective integration of the Blue Economy into development plans requires strong governance and policy coordination. National plans must align with international agreements, such as the United Nations SDGs and the Paris Agreement, as well as regional frameworks like the African Union's Blue Economy Strategy. This ensures that national priorities contribute to global sustainability efforts.

Governance structures must also foster inter-ministerial collaboration, as the Blue Economy spans multiple sectors, including fisheries, energy, tourism, and environmental conservation. For example, integrating renewable energy projects into coastal regions requires coordination between energy ministries, environmental agencies, and local governments. Transparent decision-making processes and stakeholder engagement further enhance the effectiveness of Blue Economy policies.

Challenges and Opportunities

While integrating the Blue Economy into national development plans offers significant benefits, it also presents challenges. Limited financial resources, lack of data, and inadequate institutional capacity can hinder implementation, particularly in developing nations. Moreover, balancing economic growth with environmental sustainability requires careful planning and trade-offs.

Opportunities for integration include leveraging innovative financing mechanisms such as blue bonds and public-private partnerships to fund sustainable projects. Advances in technology, such as satellite monitoring and data analytics, can support evidence-based decision-making, while capacity-building programs empower local communities and institutions to manage marine resources effectively.

By embedding the Blue Economy into national development plans, countries can create a cohesive framework for sustainable growth. This approach aligns economic, environmental, and social priorities, ensuring that marine resources are used responsibly and equitably to support long-term development goals. Through integrated planning, nations can harness the full potential of their Blue Economy while safeguarding the health of their oceans and the well-being of their communities.

Challenges in Policy Coordination and Implementation

The successful development of the Blue Economy relies on coordinated and effective policy implementation. However, given its cross-sectoral nature, which spans industries such as fisheries, energy, tourism, and conservation, achieving coherent and integrated policies is a complex task. National governments, regional bodies, and international organizations face significant challenges in aligning strategies, balancing competing priorities, and ensuring that sustainable practices are implemented on the ground. Understanding these challenges is essential to overcoming them and realizing the full potential of the Blue Economy.

Fragmentation Across Sectors and Agencies

One of the primary challenges in policy coordination is the fragmentation of governance structures. The Blue Economy involves multiple sectors, each managed by distinct government departments or agencies, such as fisheries ministries, energy authorities, and environmental regulators. Without effective inter-agency collaboration, policies often lack coherence and lead to overlapping responsibilities or conflicting objectives. For example, a fisheries policy focused on maximizing catches might conflict with conservation goals aimed at protecting marine biodiversity.

The lack of centralized coordination mechanisms exacerbates these issues, resulting in inefficiencies and missed opportunities for synergies. MSP has emerged as a tool to address this challenge by providing an integrated framework for managing ocean resources. However, its adoption and effective use require strong institutional commitment and technical capacity, which are often lacking in many countries.

Balancing Economic Growth and Environmental Sustainability

Another significant challenge is balancing the economic development goals of the Blue Economy with the need for environmental conservation. Industries such as offshore energy, shipping, and aquaculture drive economic growth but can have detrimental impacts on marine ecosystems if not managed sustainably. Policymakers often face pressure to prioritize short-term

43

economic gains over long-term ecological health, particularly in countries reliant on marine resources for revenue and employment.

This trade-off is further complicated by inadequate data and monitoring systems, which hinder the ability to assess the environmental impacts of economic activities accurately. Without reliable data, policymakers struggle to make informed decisions that balance economic and environmental priorities. Furthermore, insufficient enforcement of environmental regulations undermines efforts to ensure sustainable practices in ocean-based industries.

Limited Capacity and Resources

Many countries, particularly developing nations, face capacity constraints that impede effective policy coordination and implementation. Limited technical expertise, inadequate funding, and weak institutional frameworks often result in poorly designed or poorly enforced policies. For instance, the inability to monitor IUU fishing due to a lack of surveillance systems and trained personnel undermines efforts to achieve sustainable fisheries management.

Capacity challenges are also evident in regional and international contexts, where countries must align their national policies with global agreements such as the United Nations SDGs or the Paris Agreement. Developing the institutional capacity to implement and monitor these commitments requires significant investment in human resources, technology, and infrastructure, which many nations struggle to secure.

Conflicting Stakeholder Interests

The diverse range of stakeholders involved in the Blue Economy— government agencies, private sector entities, local communities, and environmental organizations—often have competing interests. For example, businesses may prioritize profit maximization, while environmental groups advocate for stricter conservation measures.

Coastal communities, on the other hand, may seek greater access to resources to support their livelihoods.

Reconciling these conflicting interests is a major challenge for policymakers. Inclusive decision-making processes, such as stakeholder consultations and public-private partnerships, are essential to building consensus and ensuring that policies are equitable and representative. However, these processes can be time-consuming and resource-intensive, and their outcomes may not always satisfy all parties.

Transboundary Challenges

Marine ecosystems and resources often span national borders, requiring regional and international cooperation for effective management. Transboundary issues such as overfishing, pollution, and maritime security present unique challenges for policy coordination. Disputes over jurisdictional boundaries or access to shared resources can hinder collaborative efforts, while varying levels of capacity and governance among nations complicate the implementation of joint initiatives.

Regional frameworks, such as the African Union's Blue Economy Strategy or the European Union's Integrated Maritime Policy, aim to address these challenges by fostering collaboration and harmonizing policies. However, differences in political priorities, economic interests, and institutional capacities can impede progress, requiring sustained diplomatic efforts and capacity-building support.

Navigating Complex Legal and Regulatory Frameworks

The Blue Economy operates within a complex legal and regulatory environment that includes international agreements, regional frameworks, and national laws. Ensuring compliance and alignment across these levels is a significant challenge for policymakers. Inconsistent interpretation or enforcement of international agreements, such as the UNCLOS, can create uncertainty and undermine effective governance.

To address this, countries must establish clear legal frameworks that integrate international obligations into domestic law while providing consistent guidelines for implementation. However, this process requires technical expertise, political will, and financial resources, which are often lacking in many contexts.

By addressing these challenges through improved governance structures, enhanced capacity, and inclusive decision-making, policymakers can create a cohesive framework for the Blue Economy that balances economic growth, environmental sustainability, and social equity. Tackling these obstacles is critical to ensuring that the Blue Economy delivers on its promise of sustainable development for all.

Chapter 4: Financing the Blue Economy

The transition to a sustainable Blue Economy requires significant financial investments to support innovation, infrastructure, and conservation efforts. This chapter explores the key funding mechanisms driving the Blue Economy, including public and private sector contributions, innovative tools like blue bonds, and the role of international partnerships. It also examines challenges in mobilizing and allocating resources to balance economic growth with environmental sustainability.

Role of Public and Private Investments in Blue Growth

Public and private investments play a critical role in fostering Blue Growth, enabling the sustainable development of ocean-based industries while addressing environmental and social challenges. These investments provide the financial resources necessary to develop infrastructure, advance technology, and implement conservation initiatives that align with the principles of the Blue Economy. By leveraging both public funding and private capital, countries can drive economic growth in marine sectors while ensuring long-term sustainability.

Public Sector Investments

Governments are key drivers of Blue Growth, providing funding, policy direction, and institutional support for sustainable ocean-based activities. Public investments often focus on building foundational infrastructure, such as ports, renewable energy installations, and aquaculture facilities, which are essential for economic development in coastal and marine regions. For example, government-backed renewable energy projects, like offshore wind farms, not only create jobs and stimulate economic activity but also contribute to climate goals by reducing greenhouse gas emissions.

Public funding also supports marine conservation and ecosystem restoration efforts, such as the establishment of MPAs and the rehabilitation of degraded habitats like coral reefs and mangroves. These initiatives preserve biodiversity, enhance fisheries, and protect coastal communities from climate impacts, creating a strong foundation for sustainable economic activities.

Moreover, governments play a pivotal role in research and development (R&D) for the Blue Economy. By funding scientific studies and technological innovations, public investments enable the exploration of new opportunities, such as marine biotechnology and precision aquaculture. National governments also provide financial support for capacity-building programs, empowering local communities to participate in and benefit from Blue Growth initiatives.

Private Sector Investments

The private sector is increasingly recognizing the economic potential of the Blue Economy, driving investments across a wide range of industries, including shipping, aquaculture, tourism, and renewable energy. Private capital accelerates innovation, bringing cutting-edge technologies to market and scaling sustainable business models. For instance, advancements in autonomous shipping technologies and renewable energy solutions have been fueled by private investment.

Private companies also play a vital role in financing sustainable fisheries and aquaculture projects. Impact investors, venture capitalists, and large corporations are funding initiatives that reduce environmental impacts while enhancing productivity. This includes investments in sustainable feed alternatives, water quality monitoring systems, and low-impact farming methods.

Corporate social responsibility (CSR) and environmental, social, and governance (ESG) considerations further incentivize private sector involvement in Blue Growth. Companies are increasingly integrating sustainability into their operations and investments to meet consumer demands, comply with regulations, and reduce reputational risks. For example, firms in the shipping industry are adopting cleaner technologies and more efficient logistics to minimize their environmental footprint while remaining competitive.

Public-Private Partnerships

Public-private partnerships (PPPs) serve as a critical mechanism for mobilizing resources and sharing risks in Blue Growth initiatives. These collaborations leverage the strengths of both sectors: the public sector's regulatory and policy framework combined with the private sector's financial resources and technological expertise. For example, PPPs are instrumental in developing large-scale renewable energy projects, such as offshore wind farms, where private investment is bolstered by public subsidies or guarantees.

PPPs are also effective in financing infrastructure projects, such as the construction of green ports and eco-tourism facilities. These partnerships ensure that developments align with sustainability goals while providing significant economic benefits to local communities. Additionally, they foster innovation by creating platforms for knowledge sharing and joint research between public institutions and private companies.

Challenges and Opportunities

Despite their critical role, public and private investments in the Blue Economy face several challenges. Limited financial resources, high initial costs, and uncertainties around returns can deter investment, particularly in developing nations. Addressing these barriers requires innovative financing mechanisms, such as blue bonds, blended finance, and risk-sharing agreements, to attract capital and reduce risks.

The increasing alignment of financial flows with sustainability objectives presents a significant opportunity for scaling Blue Growth. Initiatives like ESG investing, green finance, and carbon markets are channeling funds into projects that balance economic growth with environmental conservation. By aligning public and private investments, the Blue Economy can unlock its full potential, fostering sustainable development for present and future generations.

Blue Bonds and Impact Investing: Innovative Financing Mechanisms

Innovative financing mechanisms are essential for mobilizing the capital needed to support sustainable development in the Blue Economy.

Blue Bonds and Impact Investing

Blue bonds and impact investing are two innovative financing mechanisms driving the sustainable development of the Blue Economy. By channeling resources into projects that align with environmental, social, and economic objectives, these tools provide critical capital for preserving marine ecosystems, supporting coastal communities, and fostering sustainable ocean-based industries. Both mechanisms offer scalable solutions to address the funding gap for achieving global sustainability goals while delivering measurable environmental and social benefits.

Blue bonds are debt instruments designed to raise capital for projects that protect and restore marine and coastal ecosystems. Modeled after green bonds, blue bonds are issued by governments, development banks, or private organizations to fund initiatives such as marine conservation, sustainable fisheries, and renewable energy development. Investors who purchase blue bonds provide upfront capital, which is repaid over time with interest, creating a win-win scenario for financial returns and environmental impact.

One of the most notable examples of blue bonds is the issuance by the Republic of Seychelles in 2018. This groundbreaking initiative raised $15 million to fund the country's marine conservation efforts, including the expansion of MPAs and the development of sustainable fisheries. The Seychelles blue bond highlighted the potential for such instruments to attract global investors while addressing critical ocean-related challenges.

Blue bonds are particularly effective in mobilizing resources for countries with significant marine resources but limited financial capacity. SIDs and coastal nations can leverage blue bonds to finance long-term sustainability initiatives, such as coral reef restoration or mangrove rehabilitation, that benefit both ecosystems and local communities. These bonds also align with global frameworks like the SDGs, particularly SDG 14 (Life Below Water) and SDG 13 (Climate Action).

Despite their promise, the adoption of blue bonds faces challenges, including the need for robust monitoring and evaluation frameworks to ensure transparency and accountability. Investors require clear metrics to assess the impact of funded projects, making the establishment of standardized reporting mechanisms essential for scaling blue bonds globally.

Impact Investing: Balancing Returns with Sustainability

Impact investing represents another powerful tool for financing the Blue Economy, targeting investments that generate both financial returns and measurable social or environmental benefits. Unlike traditional investments, impact investing explicitly aims to address challenges such as biodiversity loss, climate change, and social inequities while ensuring profitability. This dual focus has made impact investing a key driver of innovation and sustainability in ocean-based industries.

In the context of the Blue Economy, impact investors fund projects across sectors such as sustainable aquaculture, renewable energy, and marine biotechnology. For example, investments in seaweed farming not only provide a sustainable source of food and biofuels but also contribute to carbon sequestration and marine ecosystem health. Similarly, impact investing in clean shipping technologies helps reduce greenhouse gas emissions while enhancing the efficiency of global trade.

Institutional investors, such as pension funds and insurance companies, are increasingly participating in impact investing, recognizing the long-term value of sustainable projects. Private equity firms and venture capitalists are also entering the Blue Economy space, supporting early-stage companies that develop innovative solutions for ocean-related challenges. This influx of capital fosters the growth of sustainable businesses and accelerates the transition to greener practices in traditional industries.

One of the strengths of impact investing is its flexibility, allowing investors to target specific outcomes based on their priorities. For instance, some investors focus on social equity by funding initiatives that empower small-scale fishers or coastal communities, while others prioritize environmental conservation through investments in habitat restoration or pollution reduction.

However, challenges remain in scaling impact investing for the Blue Economy. The lack of standardized impact measurement tools makes it difficult to compare investments and assess their effectiveness. Addressing this gap requires the development of consistent metrics and reporting frameworks, enabling investors to make informed decisions and track the progress of their investments over time.

Synergies and Potential for Growth

Blue bonds and impact investing are complementary tools that can unlock significant financial resources for the Blue Economy. By addressing different aspects of sustainable development—long-term funding through bonds and targeted, outcome-focused investments— they create opportunities for governments, businesses, and communities to collaborate on shared goals. Expanding the use of these mechanisms will require innovative partnerships, capacity-building efforts, and robust governance to ensure their success in driving sustainable Blue Growth.

Debt-for-Nature Swaps

Debt-for-nature swaps are innovative financial instruments that offer a win-win solution for countries facing significant debt burdens and environmental challenges. These agreements allow nations to restructure or reduce their external debt in exchange for commitments to invest in conservation and sustainable development. In the context of the Blue Economy, debt-for-nature swaps have emerged as a powerful tool for protecting marine ecosystems, supporting coastal livelihoods, and advancing global sustainability goals.

How Debt-for-Nature Swaps Work

Debt-for-nature swaps typically involve three parties: the debtor country, a creditor (such as a government or financial institution), and a third-party organization (such as an environmental NGO or development agency). Under these agreements, the creditor agrees to forgive a portion of the debtor's external debt or reduce the repayment terms. In return, the debtor country pledges to use the savings to fund conservation initiatives, such as establishing MPAs, restoring coastal habitats, or implementing sustainable fisheries management.

For example, in a typical swap, an international NGO might purchase debt from a creditor at a discounted rate. The debtor country then repays the NGO in local currency, with the funds allocated to conservation projects within its borders. This arrangement not only eases the country's debt burden but also channels much-needed resources into environmental protection.

Debt-for-nature swaps can be structured in various ways to align with the priorities of the debtor country and its creditors. Some swaps focus exclusively on marine conservation, while others address broader sustainability goals, such as renewable energy development or climate adaptation. These agreements are highly customizable, making them a versatile tool for advancing the Blue Economy.

Benefits for the Blue Economy

Debt-for-nature swaps offer numerous benefits for the Blue Economy by linking financial relief with sustainable resource management. One of the primary advantages is the protection of marine biodiversity, which is critical for maintaining healthy and productive ecosystems. Swaps often fund the creation and expansion of MPAs, safeguarding critical habitats for fish, corals, and other marine species. This supports sustainable fisheries and ecotourism, two key pillars of the Blue Economy.

In addition to environmental benefits, debt-for-nature swaps promote economic resilience. By investing in sustainable practices, such as mangrove restoration or low-impact aquaculture, these agreements create jobs and income opportunities for coastal communities. They also reduce the economic risks associated with overfishing, habitat destruction, and climate change, ensuring that marine resources remain viable for future generations.

For creditor nations and institutions, debt-for-nature swaps demonstrate a commitment to global sustainability while maintaining financial stability. These agreements align with international frameworks, such as the SDGs and the Paris Agreement, making them attractive options for governments and organizations seeking to contribute to environmental conservation.

Challenges and Considerations

Despite their potential, debt-for-nature swaps face several challenges that must be addressed to maximize their effectiveness. One significant barrier is the complexity of negotiating these agreements, which require coordination among multiple stakeholders with varying priorities. Creditor institutions may be reluctant to participate due to concerns about financial risks or the administrative burden of managing swaps.

Another challenge is ensuring that funds generated through swaps are used effectively and transparently. Robust monitoring and reporting mechanisms are essential to track the progress of conservation projects and verify that the agreed-upon outcomes are achieved. Without clear accountability, the impact of debt-for-nature swaps may fall short of expectations.

Additionally, the scale of debt-for-nature swaps is often limited compared to the overall debt burdens of many countries. While swaps provide targeted relief, they are unlikely to address systemic debt issues without broader fiscal reforms and international support.

Scaling Up Debt-for-Nature Swaps

To expand the use of debt-for-nature swaps, innovative partnerships and capacity-building efforts are essential. Collaboration among governments, international organizations, and financial institutions can streamline the negotiation process and increase the availability of funds. Incorporating climate adaptation and mitigation into swap agreements can further align these tools with global priorities, such as addressing rising sea levels and protecting vulnerable coastal communities.

Ultimately, debt-for-nature swaps represent a unique opportunity to align financial relief with environmental stewardship. By integrating these agreements into broader Blue Economy strategies, countries can protect their marine resources while fostering sustainable development, creating lasting benefits for both people and the planet.

Aligning Financial Instruments with SDG Objectives

Financial instruments play a pivotal role in advancing the SDGs by mobilizing capital for projects that promote sustainability, social equity, and economic growth. In the context of the Blue Economy, aligning financial tools with SDG objectives ensures that investments drive meaningful progress across critical areas such as marine conservation, poverty reduction, and climate action.

Targeting SDG Priorities Through Blue Finance

Blue finance instruments, such as blue bonds, impact investments, and debt-for-nature swaps, are tailored to address specific SDG priorities. For instance, blue bonds directly support SDG 14 (Life Below Water) by funding initiatives like MPAs and sustainable fisheries. Similarly, impact investments in renewable energy projects contribute to SDG 7 (Affordable and Clean Energy) while fostering innovation and job creation in coastal communities, aligning with SDG 8 (Decent Work and Economic Growth).

Debt-for-nature swaps provide another example of alignment, linking SDG 13 (Climate Action) and SDG 15 (Life on Land) by financing conservation efforts that mitigate climate impacts and preserve biodiversity. These instruments ensure that financial resources are channeled into projects that deliver measurable outcomes for people and the planet.

Promoting Accountability and Impact Measurement

To align financial instruments with SDG objectives effectively, robust accountability and impact measurement frameworks are essential. Investors and stakeholders require clear metrics to evaluate the environmental, social, and economic benefits of funded projects. Tools such as ESG reporting and SDG-focused investment indices enable transparency and help guide decision-making.

For example, ESG criteria ensure that investments in shipping or tourism adhere to sustainability standards, reducing pollution and supporting local livelihoods. By integrating these frameworks into

financial instruments, investors can better align their portfolios with
SDG priorities.

Encouraging Multisector Collaboration

Aligning financial instruments with SDGs requires collaboration
among governments, private investors, and international
organizations. PPPs leverage the strengths of different sectors,
combining public policy goals with private capital and innovation.
These partnerships are vital for scaling blue finance initiatives,
ensuring that investments contribute to global sustainability goals
while addressing local needs.

By aligning financial tools with the SDGs, the Blue Economy can
unlock its full potential, driving sustainable development while
protecting marine ecosystems and fostering equitable economic
growth.

Risks and Barriers in Financing the Blue Economy

Financing the Blue Economy presents unique challenges that stem
from its reliance on sustainability, innovation, and multi-stakeholder
collaboration. These risks and barriers can impede the flow of
investment, limiting the potential of marine industries to achieve
economic and environmental goals.

High Initial Costs and Uncertain Returns

One of the primary barriers to financing the Blue Economy is the
high upfront cost of many projects, such as offshore renewable
energy installations or marine conservation initiatives. These
projects often require significant capital investments with long
payback periods, making them less attractive to risk-averse
investors. Additionally, the profitability of certain sectors, such as
sustainable aquaculture or eco-tourism, depends on market
conditions and environmental factors, creating uncertainty around
returns.

Limited Access to Capital in Developing Nations

Many coastal and island nations, particularly in developing regions, struggle to access sufficient financial resources to invest in the Blue Economy. Limited institutional capacity, weak credit ratings, and lack of investor confidence deter both domestic and international capital. These challenges are compounded by competing priorities, such as poverty alleviation and infrastructure development, which can divert funds from marine-focused projects.

Policy and Regulatory Gaps

Inadequate policy frameworks and regulatory inconsistencies create additional risks for investors. Weak enforcement of environmental regulations, lack of clear guidelines for sustainable practices, and fragmented governance structures undermine confidence in Blue Economy projects. Without strong regulatory support, financial instruments like blue bonds or impact investments face significant implementation challenges.

Environmental and Social Risks

Environmental changes, such as rising sea levels and extreme weather events, pose significant risks to Blue Economy investments. Social risks, including inequitable resource distribution and conflicts among stakeholders, can further complicate project success. Addressing these barriers requires innovative financial mechanisms, robust governance, and targeted capacity-building efforts.

Chapter 5: Technology and Innovation in the Blue Economy

Technology and innovation are transforming the Blue Economy, offering new solutions to sustainably manage marine resources, enhance economic productivity, and address environmental challenges. This chapter explores advancements in renewable energy, aquaculture, marine biotechnology, and digital tools, highlighting their potential to drive growth while ensuring sustainability and resilience in ocean-based industries.

The Role of Technology in Enhancing Blue Economy Sectors

Technology is a driving force in the development of the Blue Economy, enabling industries to operate more efficiently, sustainably, and profitably. By integrating advanced tools and systems into sectors such as fisheries, aquaculture, renewable energy, shipping, and marine conservation, technology addresses critical challenges while unlocking new opportunities for growth and innovation.

Transforming Fisheries and Aquaculture

Technology has revolutionized fisheries and aquaculture, two cornerstone sectors of the Blue Economy. Precision fishing technologies, such as GPS-enabled tracking and sonar systems, help fishers locate target species while minimizing bycatch. These tools support sustainable practices by reducing overfishing and protecting marine biodiversity.

In aquaculture, advancements such as automated feeding systems, water quality sensors, and artificial intelligence (AI) enable farmers to optimize operations and reduce environmental impacts. IMTA systems, which combine species like fish, shellfish, and seaweed, maximize resource efficiency and minimize waste, demonstrating the potential of technology to balance productivity with sustainability.

Advancing Renewable Energy

The marine renewable energy sector has benefitted significantly from technological innovation. Offshore wind turbines, wave energy converters, and tidal energy systems are becoming more efficient and cost-effective, contributing to global clean energy goals. Floating wind turbines, in particular, are expanding the reach of offshore wind farms into deeper waters, creating opportunities for countries with limited shallow coastal areas.

Energy storage technologies and grid integration systems further enhance the reliability of marine renewable energy. These advancements ensure a stable energy supply while reducing dependency on fossil fuels, aligning the sector with climate and sustainability objectives.

Improving Shipping and Maritime Transport

The shipping industry, a critical component of global trade, is leveraging technology to reduce its environmental footprint and enhance operational efficiency. Digital tools such as route optimization software and AI-powered logistics platforms help reduce fuel consumption and emissions. The adoption of cleaner fuels, energy-efficient ship designs, and exhaust gas cleaning systems further aligns the sector with environmental goals.

Autonomous shipping technology is another area of significant potential, offering safer and more efficient maritime operations. These innovations not only reduce costs but also address labor shortages and safety concerns, ensuring the sector's long-term viability.

Driving Marine Conservation and Monitoring

Technology plays a vital role in marine conservation and the sustainable management of marine resources. Satellite imagery, drones, and underwater autonomous vehicles (UAVs) provide real-time data on ocean conditions, marine biodiversity, and illegal activities such as unregulated fishing or habitat destruction. This data supports evidence-based decision-making and strengthens enforcement efforts.

Digital platforms and geographic information systems (GIS) enhance MSP by integrating data on economic activities, ecological priorities, and social considerations. These tools ensure that ocean resources are managed sustainably, balancing development with conservation.

Unlocking Opportunities in Marine Biotechnology

Marine biotechnology, an emerging field within the Blue Economy, relies heavily on advanced technologies to explore and utilize marine organisms for innovative applications. Technologies such as high-throughput sequencing and bioinformatics enable researchers to discover bioactive compounds with potential uses in pharmaceuticals, biofuels, and sustainable materials.

For example, algae and seaweed are being harnessed to produce biodegradable plastics and alternative protein sources, reducing dependency on land-based resources. These breakthroughs demonstrate the transformative potential of technology in creating high-value products while conserving marine ecosystems.

Fostering Innovation Through Collaboration

Collaboration among governments, research institutions, and private companies is essential to fully harness the potential of technology in the Blue Economy. Partnerships foster innovation, accelerate the adoption of new tools, and ensure that technological advancements address the diverse needs of ocean-based industries. Through continued investment and cooperation, technology will remain a cornerstone of sustainable growth in the Blue Economy.

Artificial Intelligence and Data Analytics for Ocean Management

AI and data analytics are transforming ocean management by providing advanced tools to monitor, analyze, and optimize marine resource use. These technologies enable more effective decision-making, helping governments, businesses, and conservation organizations balance economic development with environmental sustainability in the Blue Economy.

Enhancing Marine Resource Monitoring

AI-powered systems play a critical role in monitoring marine ecosystems. Remote sensing technologies, coupled with AI algorithms, analyze satellite and drone imagery to track changes in ocean conditions, such as temperature, currents, and pollution levels. These tools provide real-time insights into the health of marine environments, enabling early detection of issues like coral bleaching, harmful algal blooms, or illegal fishing activities.

Underwater autonomous vehicles equipped with AI further enhance data collection by exploring areas inaccessible to humans. These devices capture high-resolution images and environmental data, offering valuable information for MSP and ecosystem protection.

Optimizing Fisheries Management

AI and data analytics are revolutionizing fisheries management by improving the precision and sustainability of operations. Predictive analytics, based on historical catch data and ocean conditions, help fishers identify optimal fishing locations while minimizing bycatch. AI algorithms also monitor fish stock levels, offering real-time assessments that inform quotas and sustainable practices.

Blockchain technology, combined with AI, enhances traceability in seafood supply chains. By tracking fish from catch to consumer, this innovation ensures compliance with sustainability standards, reduces fraud, and strengthens market transparency.

Supporting Renewable Energy and Climate Action

In renewable energy, AI optimizes the design, placement, and operation of offshore wind and tidal energy systems. Machine learning models analyze oceanographic data to predict energy output and reduce operational risks, improving efficiency and reducing costs. Additionally, AI supports climate modeling by processing vast datasets to forecast the impacts of climate change on marine ecosystems, aiding in mitigation and adaptation strategies.

Improving Decision-Making

AI and data analytics enhance decision-making across ocean industries by integrating large datasets into actionable insights. These technologies enable more efficient MSP, balancing economic, environmental, and social priorities. As AI continues to evolve, its applications in ocean management will grow, driving innovation and sustainability in the Blue Economy.

Marine Renewable Energy Technologies

Marine renewable energy technologies harness the power of oceans to provide sustainable and reliable energy solutions. These technologies are critical for transitioning to low-carbon energy systems, reducing greenhouse gas emissions, and supporting the Blue Economy's goals of sustainability and innovation.

Offshore Wind Energy

Offshore wind energy is the most developed marine renewable technology, with turbines installed in coastal and deeper waters to capture consistent and powerful wind resources. Advances in floating wind turbines are expanding the potential of offshore wind farms, allowing deployment in areas with deeper seabeds previously inaccessible to fixed-bottom structures. These innovations contribute to meeting global clean energy targets while creating jobs and stimulating local economies.

Wave Energy

Wave energy technologies convert the kinetic and potential energy of ocean waves into electricity. Devices such as point absorbers, oscillating water columns, and attenuators are being deployed to capture wave energy efficiently. While still in the early stages of commercialization, wave energy offers significant potential for coastal regions, particularly in remote and island communities that rely heavily on imported fossil fuels.

Tidal Energy

Tidal energy harnesses the predictable movement of ocean tides to generate power. Tidal barrages, tidal stream turbines, and dynamic tidal power systems are the primary technologies used. Unlike wind and solar energy, tidal energy provides consistent and reliable power due to the regularity of tidal cycles. This makes it a valuable complement to other renewable energy sources in a diversified energy mix.

Environmental Considerations and Innovation

Marine renewable energy technologies must address environmental challenges, such as impacts on marine biodiversity and ecosystem dynamics. Innovations like eco-friendly turbine designs, real-time monitoring systems, and adaptive management strategies help mitigate these effects. Strategic site selection and stakeholder engagement further ensure that energy projects align with conservation goals and local priorities.

Marine renewable energy technologies offer a pathway to sustainable energy systems, supporting climate action, energy security, and economic development in the Blue Economy. Through continued research and investment, these technologies will play a vital role in advancing global sustainability objectives.

Innovations in Sustainable Fisheries and Aquaculture

Innovations in sustainable fisheries and aquaculture are transforming these sectors into drivers of environmental stewardship and economic resilience. By integrating advanced technologies and best practices, these innovations ensure the sustainable use of marine resources while enhancing productivity and reducing ecological impacts.

Sustainable Fisheries Management

Innovative tools and practices are enabling more precise and sustainable fisheries management. Technologies such as satellite-based vessel tracking and AI-powered monitoring systems help combat IUU fishing by providing real-time data on fishing activities. These tools improve transparency and enforcement, ensuring compliance with regulations that protect fish stocks and marine ecosystems.

Smart fishing gear, such as selective nets and bycatch reduction devices, further supports sustainability by minimizing the capture of non-target species and juvenile fish. Predictive analytics, based on oceanographic and stock data, enable fishers to plan operations more effectively, reducing overfishing and optimizing resource use.

Innovations in Aquaculture

Aquaculture, the farming of aquatic organisms, has benefited significantly from advancements in technology and sustainable practices. Automated feeding systems, water quality sensors, and AI applications improve efficiency by optimizing feeding schedules and maintaining ideal environmental conditions. These innovations reduce waste, lower costs, and enhance production while minimizing the ecological footprint of farming operations.

IMTA is another breakthrough, combining the farming of fish, shellfish, and seaweed in a single system. This approach mimics natural ecosystems, where waste from one species becomes nutrients for another, improving resource efficiency and reducing pollution.

Digital Solutions and Traceability

Digital platforms and blockchain technology are revolutionizing traceability in fisheries and aquaculture. By tracking products from source to consumer, these tools ensure that seafood is sustainably sourced and meets market standards. Traceability not only supports ethical practices but also enhances consumer trust and access to premium markets.

Innovations in sustainable fisheries and aquaculture demonstrate the potential for technology and best practices to align economic growth with environmental conservation. These advancements are essential for ensuring the long-term viability of marine resources in the Blue Economy.

Leveraging Digital Tools to Monitor and Achieve SDG Targets

Digital tools play a pivotal role in accelerating progress toward the SDGs by enabling more effective monitoring, reporting, and management of resources. In the Blue Economy, these technologies provide valuable insights into ocean health, marine resource use, and socioeconomic impacts, ensuring that efforts align with global sustainability objectives. By integrating data-driven solutions into policy-making and operations, governments, businesses, and organizations can track progress and identify areas for improvement in achieving SDG targets.

Real-Time Monitoring and Data Collection

Digital tools such as satellite imagery, drones, and autonomous underwater vehicles (AUVs) are transforming how data is collected and analyzed in marine environments. These technologies provide real-time information on ocean conditions, biodiversity, and human activities, offering a comprehensive picture of marine ecosystems. For instance, satellite-based remote sensing tracks changes in sea surface temperatures, coral bleaching events, and pollution levels, directly supporting SDG 14 (Life Below Water).

In fisheries, electronic monitoring systems and AI-powered tools help track vessel activities, reducing IUU fishing. By integrating these technologies into management systems, governments can ensure compliance with sustainable practices, aligning with SDG 12 (Responsible Consumption and Production).

Improved Marine Spatial Planning

MSP relies on digital tools like GIS to balance competing demands for ocean space. GIS platforms integrate environmental, social, and economic data, enabling decision-makers to allocate marine areas for activities such as fishing, renewable energy, and conservation. This approach supports sustainable resource use while protecting vulnerable ecosystems, addressing multiple SDGs, including SDG 13 (Climate Action) and SDG 14.

Enhanced Traceability and Supply Chain Transparency

Digital tools such as blockchain and Internet of Things (IoT) devices enhance transparency in seafood supply chains. Blockchain ensures that every step of a product's journey—from harvest to consumer—is documented, supporting traceability and ethical sourcing. IoT sensors, installed on fishing vessels or aquaculture facilities, monitor environmental conditions and product quality, ensuring adherence to sustainability standards.

These innovations align with SDG 8 (Decent Work and Economic Growth) and SDG 12 by promoting fair labor practices, reducing food waste, and enabling access to premium markets that demand sustainably sourced products.

Advancing Climate Adaptation and Mitigation

Digital tools contribute to climate action (SDG 13) by improving the accuracy of climate models and forecasting tools. AI and machine learning analyze vast datasets to predict the impacts of rising sea levels, extreme weather events, and ocean acidification. These insights inform adaptation strategies, such as coastal defense planning and ecosystem restoration projects.

Renewable energy sectors also benefit from digital tools. Predictive analytics optimize the placement and operation of offshore wind turbines and tidal energy systems, enhancing efficiency and reducing environmental impacts.

Monitoring Progress Toward SDG Targets

The integration of digital tools into SDG monitoring frameworks ensures that progress is accurately tracked and reported. For example, open-access platforms such as the Global Fishing Watch use satellite data to visualize global fishing activities, enabling governments and organizations to measure progress toward SDG 14 targets. Similarly, mobile applications empower local communities to report illegal fishing or pollution incidents, fostering citizen engagement and accountability.

Big data analytics aggregate and analyze diverse datasets, providing actionable insights for policymakers. By identifying trends and gaps in implementation, these tools enable targeted interventions to accelerate progress across SDGs.

Challenges in Leveraging Digital Tools

Despite their potential, the adoption of digital tools faces challenges, particularly in developing nations. Limited technical capacity, high costs, and inadequate infrastructure hinder access to advanced technologies. Addressing these barriers requires investments in capacity building, knowledge transfer, and infrastructure development to ensure equitable access to digital solutions.

Future Opportunities

Advances in digital tools, such as AI, IoT, and blockchain, will continue to expand their applications in achieving SDG targets. By fostering collaboration among stakeholders and integrating digital solutions into governance frameworks, the Blue Economy can drive significant progress toward a sustainable future. Digital tools are not only enablers of efficient resource management but also catalysts for innovation and resilience in the face of global challenges.

Chapter 6: Sustainable Management of Ocean Resources

Effective management of ocean resources is vital for balancing economic growth with environmental conservation. This chapter examines strategies and practices for ensuring the sustainability of fisheries, marine biodiversity, and coastal ecosystems, highlighting the role of governance, technology, and community engagement in maintaining the health and productivity of our oceans.

Marine Spatial Planning: Balancing Conservation and Development

MSP is a critical tool for balancing the competing demands of conservation and development in ocean spaces. By integrating environmental, social, and economic considerations, MSP provides a structured approach to managing marine resources sustainably. It ensures that activities such as fishing, shipping, tourism, and renewable energy development coexist with efforts to protect biodiversity and maintain ecosystem health.

The Objectives of Marine Spatial Planning

The primary goal of MSP is to allocate ocean space in a way that minimizes conflicts among users while promoting sustainability. MSP supports marine conservation by identifying and protecting ecologically sensitive areas, such as coral reefs, seagrass beds, and spawning grounds. It also facilitates economic development by designating zones for activities like aquaculture, offshore wind farms, and shipping lanes, ensuring these activities do not compromise marine ecosystems.

MSP aligns closely with global sustainability goals, including SDG 14 (Life Below Water), by fostering the sustainable use of marine resources. It also supports SDG 13 (Climate Action) by enabling the strategic siting of renewable energy projects and ecosystem-based adaptation measures, such as mangrove restoration.

Key Elements of MSP

MSP relies on comprehensive data collection and stakeholder engagement. GIS and satellite technology are used to map ocean resources, assess environmental conditions, and monitor human activities. This data informs the creation of zoning plans that balance conservation priorities with economic opportunities.

Stakeholder involvement is another cornerstone of MSP. Engaging governments, industries, local communities, and environmental organizations ensures that plans reflect diverse perspectives and address the needs of all ocean users. Collaborative decision-making fosters trust and reduces conflicts, enhancing the effectiveness of MSP.

Challenges in Implementing MSP

Despite its benefits, implementing MSP faces challenges, including limited data availability, conflicting stakeholder interests, and jurisdictional complexities. In many regions, overlapping mandates among government agencies can hinder coordination. Additionally, the lack of technical capacity and funding in developing nations restricts the adoption of MSP.

Environmental uncertainties, such as climate change impacts and shifting marine ecosystems, add complexity to the planning process. MSP must be adaptive, incorporating real-time data and evolving to address emerging challenges effectively.

MSP as a Catalyst for Sustainability

MSP offers a pathway to achieving a balanced Blue Economy by integrating conservation and development objectives. Through strategic zoning and collaborative governance, MSP supports long-term ocean health, economic growth, and social equity. As ocean pressures increase, MSP will remain a critical framework for managing marine resources sustainably.

Protecting Marine Biodiversity and Ecosystems

Marine biodiversity and ecosystems are the foundation of the Blue Economy, supporting food security, livelihoods, climate regulation, and cultural heritage. Protecting these vital resources is essential for maintaining ecological balance and ensuring the long-term sustainability of ocean-based industries. Effective conservation strategies, innovative technologies, and international cooperation are critical to safeguarding marine biodiversity and ecosystems in the face of mounting environmental pressures.

Importance of Marine Biodiversity

Marine biodiversity underpins healthy ecosystems by providing essential services such as nutrient cycling, oxygen production, and carbon sequestration. Coral reefs, mangroves, and seagrass beds, for example, act as natural barriers against storm surges and coastal erosion while supporting a diverse array of species. Fisheries, aquaculture, and tourism industries depend on these ecosystems for productivity and resilience.

However, threats such as overfishing, habitat destruction, pollution, and climate change are eroding marine biodiversity at an alarming rate. Ocean acidification and warming temperatures are further exacerbating these challenges, disrupting food chains and weakening ecosystem resilience.

Marine Protected Areas

The establishment of MPAs is a cornerstone of efforts to conserve biodiversity and ecosystems. MPAs restrict harmful activities such as overfishing, dredging, and industrial development, allowing ecosystems to recover and thrive. By safeguarding critical habitats, MPAs ensure the survival of keystone species and maintain the ecological balance necessary for healthy oceans.

Effective MPAs are supported by science-based planning, community engagement, and robust enforcement mechanisms. For example, zoning within MPAs can balance conservation with sustainable use, allowing for activities like eco-tourism and regulated fishing. Expanding the global network of MPAs is essential for meeting international biodiversity targets, such as those outlined in SDG 14 (Life Below Water) and the Convention on Biological Diversity.

Innovative Conservation Approaches

Technological advancements are enhancing marine conservation efforts. Satellite monitoring, drones, and underwater autonomous vehicles enable real-time tracking of illegal activities, such as unregulated fishing or habitat destruction. Data collected through these technologies informs decision-making, strengthens enforcement, and supports adaptive management practices.

Nature-based solutions, such as restoring mangroves and coral reefs, combine conservation with economic and social benefits. These projects not only protect biodiversity but also provide carbon sequestration, enhance fisheries, and support coastal communities.

Collaborative Efforts and Policy Integration

Protecting marine biodiversity requires collaboration among governments, NGOs, industries, and local communities. International agreements, such as the UNCLOS and the CBD, provide a framework for cooperative action. Regional initiatives further strengthen cross-border efforts to address shared challenges, such as pollution and migratory species protection.

Integrating biodiversity conservation into national and regional policies ensures that economic activities align with ecological priorities. MSP and ecosystem-based management approaches balance development and conservation, promoting sustainable use of marine resources.

Challenges in Marine Biodiversity Protection

Despite progress, significant challenges remain in protecting marine biodiversity. Limited funding, inadequate enforcement, and conflicting stakeholder interests often undermine conservation efforts. Climate change and ocean acidification continue to stress ecosystems, highlighting the need for adaptive and forward-looking strategies.

Overcoming these challenges requires innovative financing mechanisms, capacity-building initiatives, and stronger governance frameworks. By prioritizing biodiversity protection, the Blue Economy can ensure the health and resilience of marine ecosystems while supporting sustainable development.

Combatting Illegal, Unreported, and Unregulated Fishing

IUU fishing is a significant threat to global marine ecosystems, sustainable fisheries, and the livelihoods of millions who depend on the ocean. IUU fishing undermines efforts to manage fish stocks sustainably, contributes to overfishing, and harms marine biodiversity. Combatting this pervasive issue is critical to achieving the objectives of the Blue Economy and aligning with global sustainability goals such as SDG 14 (Life Below Water).

The Impact of IUU Fishing

IUU fishing depletes fish stocks, disrupting marine ecosystems and threatening food security, particularly in developing countries that rely heavily on fisheries for sustenance and income. It also contributes to economic losses, with global estimates suggesting an annual cost of up to $23 billion. Beyond environmental and economic damage, IUU fishing often involves labor exploitation, further exacerbating social inequalities.

Technological Tools for Monitoring and Enforcement

Advancements in technology are revolutionizing the fight against IUU fishing. Satellite monitoring systems, such as the Automatic Identification System (AIS) and Vessel Monitoring System (VMS), track the movements of fishing vessels in real-time. These tools help identify suspicious activities, such as unauthorized entry into protected areas or unreported transshipments.

Drones and AUVs provide additional capabilities for surveillance, especially in remote or high-risk areas. Coupled with machine learning algorithms, these technologies analyze patterns to detect illegal activities more effectively. Big data analytics and AI-powered tools further enhance enforcement by processing vast datasets to identify high-risk vessels and regions.

International Cooperation and Agreements

Combating IUU fishing requires coordinated efforts at the international level. The Port State Measures Agreement (PSMA), adopted by the United Nations Food and Agriculture Organization (FAO), is a key tool in this fight. By denying port access to vessels engaged in IUU fishing, the agreement strengthens enforcement and reduces the market for illegally caught fish.

Regional initiatives, such as those led by the Indian Ocean Tuna Commission (IOTC) and the European Union, foster collaboration among nations to share intelligence, harmonize regulations, and build enforcement capacity. These efforts ensure that IUU fishing is addressed across borders, reflecting the transboundary nature of the problem.

Building Capacity and Empowering Communities

Capacity-building programs are essential for equipping governments and local authorities with the tools and knowledge to combat IUU fishing. Training for fisheries enforcement officers, investments in technology, and public awareness campaigns strengthen national and regional responses.

Empowering coastal communities also plays a vital role. Community-based monitoring systems and co-management approaches engage local stakeholders in safeguarding marine resources, enhancing compliance with regulations and promoting sustainable practices.

Promoting Sustainable Practices in Key Blue Economy Industries

The Blue Economy encompasses a wide range of industries, including fisheries, aquaculture, shipping, tourism, renewable energy, and marine biotechnology. Promoting sustainable practices in these sectors is essential for balancing economic growth with environmental conservation and social well-being. By integrating sustainability into their operations, these industries can drive long-term benefits while minimizing their ecological footprint.

Sustainable Fisheries

Fisheries are central to the Blue Economy but face significant challenges from overfishing and habitat degradation. Promoting sustainable practices in this sector involves adopting science-based management approaches, such as setting catch limits and protecting spawning areas. Technologies like electronic monitoring systems and AI-driven stock assessments ensure compliance with regulations and reduce IUU fishing.

Selective fishing gear, such as bycatch reduction devices, further supports sustainability by minimizing harm to non-target species.

Additionally, certification schemes, like the Marine Stewardship Council (MSC) label, incentivize responsible practices by providing access to premium markets and fostering consumer trust.

Sustainable Aquaculture

Aquaculture has emerged as a sustainable alternative to wild fisheries, but it must address challenges like water pollution and habitat impacts. IMTA systems, which combine species like fish, shellfish, and seaweed, enhance resource efficiency by recycling nutrients and reducing waste.

Technological advancements, such as automated feeding systems and water quality sensors, improve operational efficiency while minimizing environmental harm. Certification programs, like the Aquaculture Stewardship Council (ASC), promote best practices, ensuring that farmed seafood meets sustainability standards. These efforts align aquaculture with the broader goals of food security and ecosystem health.

Sustainable Shipping

The shipping industry, a major contributor to global trade, is working to reduce its environmental footprint through cleaner technologies and practices. Transitioning to low-carbon fuels, such as LNG and green hydrogen, is a key step toward decarbonizing the sector. Energy-efficient ship designs and digital tools for route optimization further reduce fuel consumption and emissions.

Regulatory frameworks, such as the International Maritime Organization's (IMO) strategy to reduce greenhouse gas emissions, provide guidelines for sustainable practices. Additionally, initiatives like green ports, equipped with renewable energy infrastructure and waste management systems, complement efforts to make shipping more sustainable.

Sustainable Coastal and Marine Tourism

Coastal and marine tourism generates significant revenue for the Blue Economy but can harm ecosystems through overdevelopment and pollution. Sustainable tourism models emphasize low-impact activities, such as eco-tourism, that educate visitors about marine conservation while benefiting local communities.

Certification programs, such as the Blue Flag eco-label, encourage sustainable practices in tourism operations, including waste management, energy efficiency, and biodiversity protection. Community-based tourism initiatives also promote sustainability by involving local stakeholders in decision-making and ensuring equitable distribution of economic benefits.

Renewable Energy

Marine renewable energy, including offshore wind, wave, and tidal power, offers a sustainable solution to meet global energy demands. Promoting sustainability in this sector involves minimizing the environmental impacts of energy infrastructure, such as habitat disruption and risks to marine species. Strategic site selection, eco-friendly turbine designs, and real-time monitoring systems mitigate these challenges.

The integration of marine renewable energy into coastal communities provides additional benefits, such as job creation and enhanced energy security. These projects align with global efforts to transition to low-carbon energy systems, addressing both climate and sustainability objectives.

Sustainable Marine Biotechnology

Marine biotechnology, an emerging sector within the Blue Economy, relies on the sustainable exploration of marine biodiversity. By adopting ethical sourcing practices and adhering to international regulations, such as the Nagoya Protocol, the sector ensures the equitable use of marine genetic resources.

Innovations in marine biotechnology include the development of biodegradable materials, alternative protein sources, and pharmaceuticals derived from marine organisms. These products reduce environmental impacts and support the transition to a circular economy, demonstrating the sector's potential to contribute to sustainability goals.

Cross-Cutting Strategies for Sustainability

Promoting sustainable practices across Blue Economy industries requires coordinated efforts at multiple levels. Governments play a crucial role by implementing policies and regulations that incentivize sustainability, such as tax breaks for renewable energy projects or penalties for polluting activities. PPPs foster collaboration, combining public sector oversight with private sector innovation and investment.

Education and capacity building are also vital for ensuring that stakeholders adopt sustainable practices. Training programs for workers, community engagement initiatives, and consumer awareness campaigns help embed sustainability into the fabric of Blue Economy industries. Certification schemes and eco-labels further reinforce these efforts by encouraging adherence to environmental and social standards.

Challenges and Opportunities

Despite progress, challenges remain in promoting sustainability across Blue Economy industries. High costs, limited technical capacity, and resistance to change can hinder the adoption of sustainable practices. Addressing these barriers requires innovative financing mechanisms, such as blue bonds and impact investments, to support sustainable initiatives.

Opportunities for innovation and collaboration are abundant. Advances in technology, such as AI and blockchain, enable more efficient resource management, while regional and international cooperation fosters knowledge sharing and alignment with global sustainability goals. By prioritizing sustainability, Blue Economy industries can drive inclusive growth while protecting the health of marine ecosystems for future generations.

Chapter 7: Addressing Challenges and Trade-Offs

The Blue Economy offers immense potential for sustainable development, but it also faces significant challenges and trade-offs. This chapter explores the complexities of balancing economic growth with environmental conservation, addressing competing stakeholder interests, and overcoming barriers such as governance gaps, financial constraints, and climate impacts. It highlights strategies to navigate these challenges while maximizing the benefits of the Blue Economy for all.

Overexploitation of Ocean Resources and Ecosystem Degradation

The overexploitation of ocean resources and the degradation of marine ecosystems pose significant threats to the sustainability of the Blue Economy. Unsustainable practices in industries such as fishing, mining, and tourism are depleting natural resources and disrupting ecological balance, jeopardizing the health of oceans and the livelihoods of millions who depend on them. Addressing these challenges is critical for ensuring the long-term viability of marine ecosystems and their contributions to global sustainability goals.

Causes of Overexploitation

Overexploitation stems from a combination of factors, including increased demand for marine resources, technological advancements, and weak regulatory frameworks. Industrial fishing practices, such as bottom trawling and overfishing, have significantly depleted fish stocks, with some species pushed to the brink of extinction. Similarly, deep-sea mining activities, driven by the demand for rare minerals, cause habitat destruction and disrupt deep-ocean ecosystems.

Tourism and coastal development also contribute to overexploitation. Unregulated activities, such as mass tourism in fragile coastal regions, lead to habitat destruction, pollution, and strain on local resources. Furthermore, IUU fishing exacerbates the issue, undermining conservation efforts and sustainable resource management.

Impacts on Marine Ecosystems

The degradation of marine ecosystems is one of the most significant consequences of overexploitation. Coral reefs, often referred to as the "rainforests of the sea," are highly sensitive to pressures such as overfishing and pollution. Their decline affects biodiversity, as they serve as habitats for countless marine species. Similarly, mangroves and seagrass beds, which provide critical ecosystem services such as carbon sequestration and coastal protection, are being lost at alarming rates.

The cumulative impacts of overexploitation include reduced biodiversity, disrupted food chains, and declining ecosystem services. These changes threaten the stability of marine environments and the communities that rely on them for food, income, and cultural identity.

Addressing Overexploitation

Tackling the overexploitation of ocean resources requires a combination of regulatory measures, innovative technologies, and stakeholder collaboration. Strengthening governance frameworks is essential to enforce sustainable practices and combat IUU fishing. Policies such as catch limits, seasonal bans, and MPAs help regulate resource use and allow ecosystems to recover.

Technological innovations, such as satellite monitoring, AI-driven stock assessments, and blockchain-based traceability systems, enhance transparency and accountability in marine industries. These tools enable more precise management of resources and reduce harmful practices.

Education and awareness campaigns also play a crucial role in addressing overexploitation. Engaging local communities, businesses, and consumers in sustainable practices fosters a culture of conservation and encourages compliance with regulations.

The Role of International Cooperation

Overexploitation is a transboundary issue that requires coordinated global action. International agreements, such as the UNCLOS and the CBD, provide frameworks for cooperation and resource sharing. Regional partnerships further address shared challenges, such as migratory fish stocks and pollution hotspots.

Through collective efforts, nations can align their Blue Economy strategies with sustainable resource management, ensuring the preservation of marine ecosystems for future generations. By addressing overexploitation and ecosystem degradation, the Blue Economy can fulfill its potential as a driver of sustainable development.

Climate Change Impacts on Marine Environments and Coastal Economies

Climate change is having profound and widespread effects on marine environments and coastal economies. Rising ocean temperatures, sea level rise, ocean acidification, and increased frequency of extreme weather events are disrupting marine ecosystems and the industries dependent on them. Addressing these impacts is essential for protecting biodiversity, supporting coastal communities, and ensuring the long-term sustainability of the Blue Economy.

Rising Ocean Temperatures

One of the most visible effects of climate change on marine environments is the rise in ocean temperatures. Warmer waters cause coral bleaching, a phenomenon where stressed corals expel the algae living within them, leading to a loss of vibrant ecosystems. Coral reefs, which support about 25% of marine species, are highly vulnerable to temperature fluctuations. The degradation of coral reefs not only reduces biodiversity but also harms industries such as fishing and tourism, which rely on healthy reef ecosystems.

Rising temperatures also affect fish migration patterns and reproductive cycles. Many fish species are shifting their ranges toward cooler waters, often leaving regions that rely on them for food and income vulnerable to declines in catch volume. This disruption can have severe economic implications for coastal communities that depend on fishing for their livelihoods.

Sea Level Rise and Coastal Erosion

Sea level rise is another critical climate change impact threatening coastal environments and economies. As polar ice caps melt and ocean temperatures rise, water levels are steadily increasing, leading to coastal flooding and erosion. Low-lying coastal areas, particularly in SIDs, are at heightened risk of inundation, displacing communities and threatening infrastructure, including ports, roads, and tourism facilities.

The loss of land due to erosion also impacts coastal ecosystems such as mangroves and wetlands, which provide vital services such as carbon sequestration, habitat for marine species, and protection from storm surges. The destruction of these ecosystems further exacerbates the vulnerability of coastal economies to climate change impacts.

Ocean Acidification

Ocean acidification, resulting from the absorption of excess atmospheric CO_2 by seawater, is another significant threat to marine ecosystems. The increasing acidity of oceans affects the ability of marine organisms, such as corals, shellfish, and plankton, to form shells and skeletons. This has cascading effects on food chains and the overall health of marine ecosystems.

For coastal economies, ocean acidification poses a direct threat to shellfish farming and fisheries, industries that contribute billions of dollars annually to the global economy. As the conditions for marine life become less hospitable, fish stocks and shellfish populations decline, threatening food security and livelihoods for millions of people worldwide.

Extreme Weather Events and Coastal Infrastructure

Climate change is contributing to the increased frequency and intensity of extreme weather events, including hurricanes, cyclones, and typhoons. These events cause significant damage to coastal infrastructure, including ports, roads, and homes. They also disrupt maritime shipping routes, impacting global trade and supply chains.

For coastal economies, the economic losses from extreme weather events are compounded by the costs of recovery and rebuilding. Communities that rely on tourism, fisheries, and agriculture are particularly vulnerable, as these industries are highly sensitive to weather disruptions. In many cases, repeated damage from storms leads to long-term economic instability and increased migration pressures.

Adaptation and Resilience Building

Addressing the impacts of climate change on marine environments and coastal economies requires a combination of mitigation and adaptation strategies. For marine ecosystems, creating and enforcing MPAs helps increase resilience to climate change by allowing ecosystems to recover and adapt. Restoration efforts for critical habitats such as mangroves, seagrasses, and coral reefs also enhance ecosystem services, providing natural buffers against sea level rise and extreme weather events.

For coastal economies, investing in resilient infrastructure, such as flood defenses and early warning systems, can reduce the impacts of climate-related disasters. Diversifying income sources through sustainable aquaculture, eco-tourism, and renewable energy also enhances resilience, ensuring that communities can weather the economic shocks of climate change.

Incorporating climate change considerations into MSP, fisheries management, and coastal development policies is essential to build long-term resilience and ensure the sustainability of both marine environments and coastal economies. By taking proactive measures, it is possible to mitigate the impacts of climate change while fostering the continued growth and sustainability of the Blue Economy.

Social Equity in the Blue Economy: Addressing Vulnerabilities of Coastal Communities

The Blue Economy holds immense potential for fostering economic growth and sustainability, yet its benefits must be shared equitably among all stakeholders, particularly vulnerable coastal communities. These communities, often highly dependent on marine resources for their livelihoods, face significant challenges arising from environmental degradation, climate change, and economic shifts. Ensuring social equity in the Blue Economy involves addressing these vulnerabilities and providing opportunities for marginalized populations to actively participate in and benefit from ocean-based industries.

Vulnerabilities of Coastal Communities

Coastal communities, particularly in developing countries, are among the most vulnerable to the impacts of environmental degradation and climate change. Rising sea levels, extreme weather events, and the loss of critical marine habitats, such as mangroves and coral reefs, threaten both the physical security of these communities and their economic viability. Many coastal populations rely on small-scale fisheries, aquaculture, and tourism for income, making them particularly susceptible to changes in ocean health.

Additionally, poverty and limited access to resources further exacerbate the vulnerabilities of these communities. Without access to financial services, education, or technology, many coastal dwellers struggle to adapt to the pressures of the Blue Economy. In some cases, these communities are marginalized from decision-making processes, making it harder for them to advocate for their needs and secure sustainable livelihoods.

Addressing Vulnerabilities through Inclusive Governance

One of the fundamental aspects of promoting social equity in the Blue Economy is ensuring that coastal communities have a voice in governance and decision-making processes. Participatory governance models, where local communities are involved in the planning, management, and implementation of policies, are essential for creating inclusive, sustainable solutions. By including local knowledge and perspectives, these governance structures help ensure that policies are aligned with the needs and priorities of coastal populations.

Co-management approaches, which involve collaboration between local communities, governments, and businesses, also play a key role in fostering equity. These models encourage joint responsibility for managing marine resources, ensuring that local stakeholders are not only beneficiaries but also stewards of the resources they depend on. Such approaches help build trust, improve resource management, and promote social and environmental sustainability.

Promoting Economic Opportunities and Diversification

To reduce the vulnerability of coastal communities, it is crucial to promote economic diversification. Many communities are overly reliant on a single industry, such as fishing or tourism, which can make them highly vulnerable to market fluctuations, resource depletion, and environmental changes. Providing alternative income sources can help build resilience and reduce economic risks.

Sustainable aquaculture and eco-tourism are two examples of industries that can provide viable alternatives to traditional livelihoods. By promoting environmentally responsible aquaculture practices, such as IMTA, communities can diversify their income while ensuring the sustainability of marine resources. Similarly, eco-tourism initiatives, which focus on sustainable travel experiences, can create employment opportunities while preserving marine ecosystems.

Renewable energy projects, such as offshore wind farms and tidal energy systems, also offer new opportunities for coastal communities. These projects not only provide clean energy but also create local jobs in construction, maintenance, and operations. By ensuring that these industries are developed with community input and that benefits are fairly distributed, the Blue Economy can support sustainable development and reduce inequalities.

Addressing Gender Inequality in Coastal Economies

Gender inequality remains a significant issue in many coastal communities, where women are often excluded from decision-making processes and face barriers to economic participation. In fisheries and aquaculture, for example, women often play key roles in processing, marketing, and selling seafood but have limited access to resources such as land, capital, and training. In many cases, their contributions are undervalued, and they face lower wages and poor working conditions.

To promote social equity in the Blue Economy, it is essential to address these gender disparities. Empowering women through access to education, skills training, and financial resources is critical to enabling them to participate fully in the Blue Economy. Furthermore, policies that encourage gender-sensitive approaches to fisheries management, tourism, and aquaculture can help ensure that women's voices are heard and their rights are respected.

Integrating gender considerations into marine resource management, such as promoting women's participation in co-management initiatives or providing leadership training, can lead to more equitable and effective outcomes. By supporting women in leadership roles, the Blue Economy can foster a more inclusive and diverse approach to sustainable development.

Social Protection and Capacity Building

In addition to promoting economic diversification and gender equality, social protection programs are essential to address the vulnerabilities of coastal communities. Social safety nets, such as unemployment insurance, health care, and pension schemes, can help mitigate the economic risks posed by environmental changes and market fluctuations. These programs provide a safety net for individuals and families during periods of hardship, ensuring that they can recover and rebuild.

Capacity building is also vital for empowering coastal communities to adapt to the changing dynamics of the Blue Economy. Providing education and skills development in sustainable fishing practices, marine conservation, and renewable energy can help community members transition to new, more sustainable livelihoods. Strengthening local institutions and governance systems ensures that communities can manage resources effectively and advocate for their interests.

Conflict Resolution in Ocean Use: Fisheries, Tourism, and Energy Development

Conflicts over ocean use are increasingly common as industries such as fisheries, tourism, and energy development compete for limited marine space and resources. These sectors are all vital to the global economy and the well-being of coastal communities, yet their activities often overlap, creating tensions that threaten sustainability and the livelihoods of local populations. Effective conflict resolution strategies are essential to balance the diverse needs of these industries, protect marine ecosystems, and ensure equitable benefits for all stakeholders involved.

Fisheries vs. Tourism

Fisheries and tourism are two of the most significant industries dependent on healthy marine ecosystems, yet they often come into conflict. Overfishing and destructive fishing practices can degrade the marine environment, undermining the natural attractions that support tourism, such as coral reefs and marine life. On the other hand, large-scale tourism developments, such as resorts or cruise ship terminals, can lead to habitat destruction, pollution, and overcrowding, disrupting local fish populations and fisheries.

To resolve these conflicts, effective management strategies are essential. MSP offers a solution by allocating zones for fishing, tourism, and other activities based on scientific data and stakeholder input. This integrated approach ensures that marine ecosystems are protected while allowing for the sustainable use of resources by both industries. Additionally, promoting eco-tourism and sustainable fishing practices can help align the goals of both sectors, encouraging collaboration over competition.

Stakeholder engagement is crucial in resolving these conflicts. By involving local communities, fishermen, and tourism operators in the decision-making process, stakeholders can work together to establish mutually beneficial solutions, such as sustainable tourism practices that support local economies without depleting marine resources. Furthermore, certification programs like the Marine Stewardship Council (MSC) for sustainable fisheries and eco-certifications for tourism can help promote responsible practices and create incentives for industries to work together.

Fisheries vs. Energy Development

The expansion of marine renewable energy, including offshore wind farms, tidal energy, and wave energy projects, often brings it into conflict with traditional fisheries. These energy projects can disrupt fish habitats, alter migration patterns, and create barriers to fishing areas. Conversely, fisheries can disrupt the construction and operation of energy projects if fishing activities are not adequately managed around these installations.

Conflict resolution between fisheries and energy development requires careful planning and adaptive management. Early consultation with stakeholders, including the fishing industry, energy developers, and environmental groups, is essential to identify potential conflicts before they arise. MSP can again be a useful tool to identify appropriate sites for energy installations that minimize the impact on important fishing grounds.

One potential solution to mitigate conflicts is to design energy projects in ways that minimize disruption to fish populations, such as situating wind turbines or tidal devices in less critical areas. Additionally, compensation schemes for affected fishermen, such as alternative fishing areas or financial compensation, can be part of the resolution process. Monitoring programs that track the impact of energy projects on marine life can also help to ensure that adjustments can be made as needed.

Tourism vs. Energy Development

Tourism and energy development are both vital to the economies of coastal regions, but their expansion can lead to significant environmental impacts. Large-scale energy projects, such as offshore wind farms or oil drilling platforms, can negatively affect the aesthetics of marine areas, disrupt coastal ecosystems, and diminish the attractiveness of tourism destinations. This, in turn, can result in economic losses for communities dependent on tourism.

To resolve conflicts between these sectors, it is essential to adopt strategies that balance the need for energy production with the preservation of natural and cultural resources that attract tourists. This can include zoning, buffer zones, or restrictions on energy development in sensitive or high-value tourism areas. In some cases, the construction of energy infrastructure can be timed to avoid peak tourist seasons, reducing the negative impact on local economies.

Stakeholder collaboration is critical in these cases. Engaging with local tourism operators, energy developers, and environmentalists from the outset ensures that potential conflicts are addressed early. Additionally, community-led initiatives, such as developing sustainable energy solutions that cater to the needs of the tourism industry while reducing environmental harm, can create shared value for both sectors.

Integrated Conflict Resolution Approaches

Effective conflict resolution in ocean use requires integrated approaches that address the competing demands of multiple industries while promoting sustainability. Key to this is adopting ecosystem-based management (EBM), which considers the entire marine environment and its interrelated components, including ecological, social, and economic factors. By recognizing the connections between fisheries, tourism, and energy development, EBM ensures that decisions consider the long-term health of marine ecosystems and the needs of all stakeholders.

Negotiation, mediation, and conflict management frameworks can also play an important role in resolving disputes. Neutral facilitators, such as mediators or third-party experts, can help bridge the gap between conflicting interests and find common ground. Regular communication and transparency in decision-making foster trust among stakeholders and contribute to cooperative problem-solving.

Ultimately, conflict resolution in ocean use requires a combination of sound governance, stakeholder involvement, and innovative management solutions. By fostering collaboration and seeking common solutions, it is possible to balance the competing demands of fisheries, tourism, and energy development, ensuring the sustainable and equitable use of marine resources for future generations.

Chapter 8: Measuring Progress and Impact

Effective measurement of progress and impact is essential for ensuring that the Blue Economy delivers on its promises of sustainable growth and environmental stewardship. This chapter explores the tools, indicators, and frameworks used to assess the effectiveness of Blue Economy strategies. It highlights the importance of monitoring key metrics related to marine resource management, economic performance, and social equity, providing a clear path for adapting and refining policies to achieve long-term sustainability.

Indicators for Monitoring Blue Economy Contributions to the SDGs

To ensure that the Blue Economy contributes effectively to the achievement of the United Nations SDGs, it is essential to track progress using robust indicators. These indicators allow stakeholders to measure the success of Blue Economy activities in promoting sustainable growth, protecting marine ecosystems, and enhancing social equity. By aligning with the SDGs, these indicators provide a clear framework for assessing how marine industries contribute to environmental sustainability, economic development, and social well-being.

Environmental Indicators

Environmental indicators are critical for tracking the health of marine ecosystems and the sustainability of ocean-based industries. For SDG 14 (Life Below Water), these indicators measure the status of marine biodiversity, the health of critical ecosystems, and the impacts of human activities such as overfishing and pollution.

1. **Marine Protected Areas**: The percentage of marine areas designated as MPAs is a key indicator for SDG 14. Expanding

MPAs helps conserve biodiversity, protect ecosystems, and support sustainable fisheries. Monitoring the size, coverage, and management effectiveness of MPAs ensures that they are fulfilling their conservation objectives.

2. **Fish Stock Status**: Tracking the abundance of key fish stocks is essential for assessing the sustainability of fisheries. Indicators such as the proportion of fish stocks within safe biological limits help determine whether fishing practices are sustainable and align with SDG 14 targets.

3. **Pollution Levels**: Measuring pollution levels, including plastics, nutrients, and chemical contaminants, is vital for understanding the impact of human activities on marine environments. These indicators support efforts to reduce marine pollution, a key target of SDG 14. Monitoring pollution levels also contributes to achieving SDG 12 (Responsible Consumption and Production) by promoting waste reduction strategies.

4. **Carbon Sequestration**: Indicators that measure the carbon sequestration capacity of marine ecosystems, such as mangroves, seagrasses, and coral reefs, are essential for addressing SDG 13 (Climate Action). These ecosystems play a significant role in mitigating climate change by absorbing carbon dioxide and acting as natural buffers against climate impacts.

Economic Indicators

Economic indicators measure the financial contributions of ocean-based industries, such as fisheries, aquaculture, shipping, and renewable energy. These metrics help track progress toward SDG 8 (Decent Work and Economic Growth) and SDG 9 (Industry, Innovation, and Infrastructure).

1. **Contribution of Blue Economy Sectors to GDP**: Monitoring the economic output of key Blue Economy sectors, including sustainable fisheries, renewable energy, and tourism, allows governments to

assess the overall economic impact of the Blue Economy. This indicator helps track progress in creating sustainable industries and supporting economic growth.

2. **Employment in Sustainable Ocean-Based Industries**: Employment indicators, including the number of jobs created in sustainable fisheries, aquaculture, renewable energy, and eco-tourism, are essential for tracking SDG 8. These indicators reflect the contribution of the Blue Economy to decent work and income generation, particularly in coastal and island communities.

3. **Revenue from Sustainable Aquaculture and Fisheries**: Revenue generated from sustainable fisheries and aquaculture operations is an important economic indicator. By tracking revenue, it is possible to assess the financial viability and sustainability of these industries and their alignment with SDG 14 (Life Below Water) and SDG 12 (Responsible Consumption and Production).

Social Indicators

Social indicators are crucial for ensuring that the benefits of the Blue Economy are distributed equitably and contribute to reducing poverty and promoting social inclusion, in line with SDG 1 (No Poverty) and SDG 10 (Reduced Inequalities).

1. **Access to Education and Training in Marine Industries**: The number of individuals, particularly women and marginalized groups, receiving education and training in marine resource management and sustainable industries is an important indicator for achieving SDG 4 (Quality Education) and SDG 5 (Gender Equality). Capacity-building efforts empower local communities and improve participation in decision-making processes.

2. **Livelihoods Dependent on Sustainable Marine Resources**: Indicators that track the number of people whose livelihoods are dependent on sustainable ocean-based industries, such as sustainable fishing or eco-tourism, are essential for understanding the social

impact of the Blue Economy. These indicators help assess whether Blue Economy initiatives are contributing to poverty reduction and social inclusion.

3. **Gender Equality in Ocean-Based Industries**: Gender-disaggregated data on participation, leadership, and income in ocean-based industries are key to ensuring that women and other underrepresented groups benefit equitably from the Blue Economy. Tracking gender equality indicators in fisheries, aquaculture, and renewable energy can help ensure that SDG 5 (Gender Equality) is addressed.

Integration of Data for Policy Development

These indicators must be integrated into national and regional policy frameworks to ensure that the Blue Economy's contributions to the SDGs are effectively monitored. Data collected through these indicators must be analyzed, communicated, and used to inform policy decisions, enabling governments to make evidence-based adjustments to Blue Economy strategies. Regular reporting on these indicators through national and international platforms, such as the United Nations SDG indicators framework, ensures transparency and accountability in the pursuit of sustainable ocean management.

Tools and Frameworks for Assessing Sustainability

Assessing the sustainability of Blue Economy activities is crucial for ensuring that economic growth does not come at the expense of environmental health and social well-being. To effectively monitor and evaluate sustainability, a range of tools and frameworks have been developed to provide comprehensive assessments of ocean-based industries. These tools help track performance, guide decision-making, and facilitate adaptive management to promote long-term sustainability.

Marine Spatial Planning

MSP is a critical tool for assessing and managing the sustainable use of ocean resources. MSP involves the spatial allocation of ocean space to various activities, such as fisheries, shipping, tourism, and renewable energy, while considering environmental, social, and economic factors. By integrating ecosystem services, biodiversity conservation, and human activities, MSP helps to minimize conflicts between sectors and maximize the benefits of marine resources.

MSP is a participatory process, often involving stakeholders such as local communities, governments, industry representatives, and environmental groups. This inclusive approach ensures that sustainability considerations are integrated into decision-making and that management strategies balance conservation goals with economic growth. As a framework, MSP supports adaptive management, enabling continuous improvement in the face of new challenges such as climate change and overexploitation.

Ecosystem-Based Management

EBM is another key framework for assessing sustainability in the Blue Economy. Unlike traditional resource management approaches that focus on individual species or sectors, EBM takes a holistic view of entire ecosystems, recognizing the interdependencies among species, habitats, and human activities. By focusing on the health and resilience of ecosystems, EBM seeks to preserve the functions and services provided by marine and coastal environments, such as carbon sequestration, flood protection, and biodiversity.

EBM requires comprehensive data collection, including monitoring the state of ecosystems, assessing the impacts of human activities, and evaluating the effectiveness of management measures. This approach supports long-term sustainability by accounting for cumulative and indirect impacts, ensuring that economic activities are aligned with the capacity of ecosystems to support them. EBM is particularly important in managing MPAs and conserving critical habitats like mangroves, seagrasses, and coral reefs.

Sustainability Indicators

Sustainability indicators are essential for tracking progress toward sustainable development goals and evaluating the environmental, economic, and social performance of Blue Economy sectors. These indicators allow policymakers and stakeholders to monitor trends, identify areas for improvement, and make data-driven decisions.

Environmental indicators, such as biodiversity indices, fish stock assessments, and pollution levels, measure the health of marine ecosystems and the impact of human activities. Economic indicators, such as GDP contribution from ocean-based industries, employment rates in sustainable sectors, and revenue from sustainable fisheries, assess the economic viability of the Blue Economy. Social indicators, including access to education, equitable income distribution, and gender equality in marine industries, help monitor the social sustainability of Blue Economy activities.

By integrating environmental, economic, and social indicators, sustainability assessments provide a comprehensive picture of how Blue Economy activities are contributing to the achievement of global sustainability targets, such as the United Nations SDGs.

Life Cycle Assessment

Life Cycle Assessment (LCA) is a tool for evaluating the environmental impacts of products, processes, or services throughout their entire life cycle—from raw material extraction and production to consumption and disposal. In the context of the Blue Economy, LCA can be applied to industries such as fisheries, aquaculture, shipping, and renewable energy to assess the environmental footprint of their operations.

For example, LCA can be used to compare the environmental impacts of different types of fish farming systems, such as open-net pens versus land-based recirculating systems, or to evaluate the carbon footprint of various renewable energy technologies like offshore wind farms and tidal energy systems. LCA helps identify areas where improvements can be made to reduce resource consumption, minimize waste, and lower carbon emissions, contributing to the overall sustainability of Blue Economy sectors.

Integrated Reporting and ESG Frameworks

Integrated reporting and ESG frameworks are increasingly being used by companies within the Blue Economy to assess and communicate their sustainability performance. These frameworks provide a comprehensive view of how businesses manage environmental, social, and governance risks and opportunities.

ESG reporting includes metrics related to resource use, waste management, labor practices, community engagement, and corporate governance. By disclosing these factors, businesses can demonstrate their commitment to sustainability and align with global standards, such as the Global Reporting Initiative (GRI) or the UN Principles for Responsible Investment (PRI). Integrated reporting goes a step further by linking ESG factors with financial performance, providing investors with a clear picture of how sustainability practices contribute to long-term profitability.

These tools help companies within the Blue Economy improve transparency, manage risks, and enhance their reputation among investors, regulators, and consumers, thereby supporting the transition toward more sustainable practices across industries.

Role of Global Reporting Initiatives and Partnerships

Global reporting initiatives and partnerships play a pivotal role in advancing sustainability in the Blue Economy by providing frameworks, standards, and collaborative platforms that guide businesses, governments, and other stakeholders in measuring and reporting their ESG impacts. These initiatives foster transparency, accountability, and best practices, ensuring that Blue Economy activities contribute to achieving the United Nations SDGs and broader sustainability objectives.

Global Reporting Initiative (GRI)

The Global Reporting Initiative (GRI) is one of the most widely used frameworks for sustainability reporting, offering guidelines for businesses to disclose their ESG impacts. GRI's comprehensive standards enable organizations in the Blue Economy to communicate their sustainability performance in a consistent, transparent, and comparable manner. This includes reporting on environmental impacts, such as marine pollution and resource depletion, as well as social factors like labor rights and community engagement.

For Blue Economy sectors such as fisheries, aquaculture, and shipping, GRI provides a platform for reporting on key sustainability issues, such as sustainable sourcing, supply chain management, and emissions reduction. By aligning with GRI standards, companies demonstrate their commitment to sustainable practices and build trust with investors, consumers, and regulators. Furthermore, GRI reporting encourages organizations to set measurable targets and track progress over time, creating a clear pathway toward improving their environmental and social outcomes.

Sustainability Accounting Standards Board (SASB)

The Sustainability Accounting Standards Board (SASB) is another important reporting initiative that helps organizations in the Blue Economy disclose financially material ESG factors to investors. SASB provides industry-specific standards that are tailored to the unique challenges and risks faced by various sectors. For example, the SASB standards for marine transportation focus on issues such as fuel efficiency, greenhouse gas emissions, and waste management.

By utilizing SASB standards, businesses can improve their engagement with investors, demonstrating how their activities contribute to long-term value creation while mitigating environmental and social risks. This reporting framework emphasizes the integration of sustainability into business strategy, ensuring that companies in the Blue Economy address both financial and non-financial performance metrics.

United Nations Global Compact (UNGC)

The United Nations Global Compact (UNGC) is a voluntary initiative that encourages companies to align their operations with ten principles related to human rights, labor standards, the environment, and anti-corruption. By signing the UNGC, businesses in the Blue Economy commit to adhering to these principles and reporting on their progress.

UNGC's focus on environmental responsibility, particularly in areas like climate change, biodiversity conservation, and sustainable water use, is directly relevant to the Blue Economy. Companies in sectors like fisheries, shipping, and renewable energy can align their operations with the UNGC's environmental principles, reporting their contributions to SDG 13 (Climate Action) and SDG 14 (Life Below Water).

Furthermore, the UNGC's annual Communication on Progress (COP) provides a framework for businesses to report on their sustainability efforts and demonstrate their commitment to responsible practices. This fosters greater corporate accountability and transparency, encouraging companies to continuously improve their ESG performance.

Partnerships for the SDGs

Partnerships play a central role in driving the Blue Economy towards sustainability. Multilateral initiatives, such as the Global Partnership for Oceans (GPO), bring together governments, businesses, NGOs, and international organizations to address ocean-related challenges. These partnerships foster collaboration across sectors and regions, creating synergies that amplify the collective impact on marine conservation and sustainable use of ocean resources.

For instance, the GPO has focused on sustainable fisheries management, marine pollution, and MSP, promoting cross-sectoral collaboration to achieve SDG 14 (Life Below Water). These partnerships often provide financial resources, technical expertise, and policy support to facilitate the adoption of sustainable practices in ocean industries. By participating in such partnerships, businesses in the Blue Economy can contribute to shared goals while enhancing their sustainability performance.

Similarly, partnerships like the Global Environmental Facility (GEF) or the Green Climate Fund (GCF) provide funding and technical assistance for projects that address environmental and climate-related challenges in coastal and marine ecosystems. These partnerships enable countries and businesses to access resources that support the transition to a sustainable Blue Economy.

The Role of Industry-Specific Sustainability Initiatives

In addition to global frameworks like GRI and UNGC, industry-specific sustainability initiatives also play a crucial role in advancing sustainable practices within the Blue Economy. For example, the Marine Stewardship Council (MSC) certification program sets standards for sustainable fisheries management, promoting practices that reduce overfishing and protect marine biodiversity.

Similarly, the Aquaculture Stewardship Council (ASC) certifies aquaculture operations that meet stringent environmental and social criteria, ensuring that farmed seafood is produced sustainably. These certifications offer transparency and help consumers make informed choices, incentivizing businesses to adopt sustainable practices that align with the broader objectives of the Blue Economy.

Adaptive Management for Continual Improvement

Adaptive management is a dynamic approach to resource management that enables continuous learning and improvement in the face of uncertainty. This management strategy is particularly relevant to the Blue Economy, where ecosystems and industries are subject to change due to environmental pressures, economic shifts, and technological advancements. By incorporating flexibility and responsiveness into decision-making processes, adaptive management ensures that strategies remain effective over time, promoting sustainability and resilience in marine and coastal sectors.

Principles of Adaptive Management

At its core, adaptive management is based on the principle that resource management must be flexible and iterative, allowing for ongoing adjustments in response to new information or changing conditions. It involves setting clear goals, monitoring progress, evaluating outcomes, and modifying actions when necessary. This process helps ensure that management strategies are not rigid but are instead able to evolve based on real-world observations, feedback, and scientific research.

Key principles of adaptive management include:

1. **Monitoring and Data Collection**: Continuous monitoring of environmental, social, and economic factors is essential to understanding the effectiveness of management strategies. In the context of the Blue Economy, this could involve tracking fish populations, ecosystem health, or the impact of renewable energy projects.

2. **Learning and Feedback Loops**: Adaptive management emphasizes the importance of learning from past actions. Feedback loops allow for the evaluation of outcomes against objectives, enabling managers to adjust strategies based on observed results. This iterative process helps refine policies and practices over time.

3. **Flexibility**: Flexibility is a hallmark of adaptive management, ensuring that strategies can be altered as new information becomes available or as circumstances change. This is particularly important in the Blue Economy, where uncertainty surrounding ocean ecosystems and human activities is high.

4. **Stakeholder Involvement**: Engaging stakeholders—such as local communities, industry representatives, and environmental groups—is crucial to adaptive management. Stakeholders contribute valuable local knowledge and help ensure that management actions are inclusive and reflective of diverse needs.

Application in the Blue Economy

In the Blue Economy, adaptive management provides a framework for sustainable use of marine resources while responding to emerging challenges such as climate change, overfishing, and pollution. This approach is applied across various sectors, including fisheries, aquaculture, marine conservation, and renewable energy.

1. **Fisheries Management**: Adaptive management in fisheries involves regularly assessing fish stocks, reviewing catch limits, and adjusting harvesting practices based on new scientific data. For instance, in response to declining fish populations, management strategies might include stricter quotas, closed seasons, or the establishment of no-catch zones. By continuously monitoring fish stocks and adjusting management practices, fisheries can avoid overexploitation and ensure long-term sustainability.

2. **Aquaculture Practices**: In aquaculture, adaptive management helps address issues such as water quality, disease management, and feed efficiency. As conditions change, such as rising water temperatures or shifting environmental conditions, aquaculture operations can modify practices to reduce environmental impacts. Monitoring systems that track water quality, fish health, and feed conversion ratios allow for timely adjustments to improve efficiency and sustainability.

3. **Marine Conservation**: MPAs and other conservation strategies benefit from adaptive management by ensuring that they can respond to shifts in biodiversity, climate conditions, and human activities. For example, the size or boundaries of an MPA may be adjusted based on observed changes in species migration patterns or the health of ecosystems. Adaptive management ensures that conservation efforts remain effective and that ecosystems continue to thrive.

4. **Renewable Energy**: As offshore renewable energy projects, such as wind farms or tidal energy systems, are developed, adaptive management allows developers to adjust plans based on environmental monitoring. For example, the placement of wind turbines can be adjusted to minimize impacts on marine ecosystems or migratory species. Regular monitoring of environmental impacts, such as changes in water quality, noise pollution, or effects on marine life, enables continuous improvement and alignment with sustainability goals.

Challenges and Barriers to Implementation

Despite its benefits, implementing adaptive management in the Blue Economy can be challenging. One significant barrier is the lack of reliable data. Many marine ecosystems and ocean resources remain poorly understood, making it difficult to set baseline measurements and track progress. Overcoming this requires investment in research, data collection, and monitoring infrastructure.

Another challenge is the need for coordination among multiple stakeholders, each with their own interests and priorities. Effective adaptive management requires strong governance structures and transparent decision-making processes to ensure that all stakeholders are engaged and that decisions reflect a balance of ecological, economic, and social goals.

In some cases, institutional inertia or resistance to change can also hinder the adoption of adaptive management strategies. Many traditional management practices are rigid and focused on short-term outcomes, making it difficult to adopt more flexible, long-term approaches.

Benefits of Adaptive Management

Despite these challenges, the benefits of adaptive management in the Blue Economy are significant. It promotes resilience by allowing systems to respond to dynamic and unpredictable changes in the environment. It also supports the integration of new scientific knowledge and technological advances into management practices, ensuring that strategies remain relevant and effective.

Furthermore, adaptive management fosters stakeholder trust by providing a transparent, collaborative approach to decision-making. As stakeholders see that their input is valued and that management strategies are responsive to changing conditions, they are more likely to support and engage in sustainable practices.

Ultimately, adaptive management is essential for achieving the goals of the Blue Economy, ensuring that marine resources are used sustainably while promoting economic growth and social equity. By continuously learning and adapting to new challenges, the Blue Economy can remain resilient and sustainable in the face of evolving environmental and economic conditions.

Conclusion: Toward a Sustainable Blue Economy

The journey toward a sustainable Blue Economy requires the integration of environmental stewardship, economic growth, and social equity. This chapter synthesizes the key insights from the previous discussions, emphasizing the need for innovative policies, collaboration across sectors, and continuous monitoring to achieve long-term sustainability. By addressing challenges, embracing new technologies, and fostering inclusive governance, the Blue Economy can unlock its full potential to protect ocean resources while contributing to global prosperity and resilience.

The Imperative of Strengthening Blue Economy Governance and Policy

Effective governance and robust policy frameworks are essential for the sustainable development of the Blue Economy. As ocean-based industries expand and marine ecosystems face growing pressures, there is an urgent need to strengthen governance structures and policy interventions that ensure the balance between economic growth, environmental protection, and social equity.

Coordinated Governance Frameworks

Governance in the Blue Economy must be coordinated across multiple levels—local, national, regional, and international—to address the transboundary nature of marine resources. Fragmented governance, where multiple agencies manage different sectors of the ocean economy without coordination, can lead to conflicting policies, inefficiencies, and overexploitation of marine resources. Integrated and ecosystem-based approaches to governance are critical for aligning the diverse interests of stakeholders, including fisheries, tourism, renewable energy, and conservation.

A key aspect of strengthening governance is the creation of collaborative frameworks that bring together governments, the private sector, local communities, and non-governmental organizations (NGOs). These partnerships can help to design policies that are not only sustainable but also inclusive, ensuring that all voices are heard and that the benefits of the Blue Economy are equitably distributed.

Policy Coherence and Long-Term Vision

Governance frameworks must be backed by coherent and forward-thinking policies. Policies that support the Blue Economy should not only focus on short-term goals but also align with long-term sustainability objectives, such as climate change mitigation, ocean conservation, and poverty reduction. To achieve these objectives, policies must integrate environmental protection with economic incentives, promoting industries like sustainable fisheries, aquaculture, and renewable energy while minimizing their ecological footprint.

Furthermore, policies should be flexible enough to adapt to emerging challenges, including the effects of climate change, overfishing, and new technological developments. Policymakers need to account for uncertainty and variability, creating adaptive frameworks that allow for adjustments based on new data, monitoring outcomes, and scientific research.

Strengthening International Cooperation

The global nature of the oceans necessitates international cooperation to address challenges that transcend national borders, such as marine pollution, illegal fishing, and biodiversity loss. Strengthening international agreements, such as the UNCLOS, and supporting global initiatives like the SDGs, are vital for ensuring the global governance of the Blue Economy is effective and cohesive.

By fostering cross-border partnerships and supporting international conventions, nations can work together to address the most pressing ocean-related issues while aligning their policies with global sustainability targets.

Integrating Traditional Knowledge and Modern Innovations

The integration of traditional knowledge with modern innovations is crucial for achieving sustainability in the Blue Economy. Indigenous and local communities have long relied on marine ecosystems for their livelihoods, and their deep understanding of ocean resources, developed over generations, offers valuable insights into sustainable practices. Combining this traditional knowledge with modern technologies and scientific innovations can lead to more effective management of marine resources, fostering resilience and sustainability in ocean-based industries.

Value of Traditional Knowledge

Traditional knowledge encompasses the practices, observations, and ecological understanding passed down through generations. In coastal and island communities, this knowledge is intimately linked with the natural world and often includes sustainable fishing practices, seasonal migration patterns of marine species, and ecosystem management techniques such as rotational harvesting. This knowledge is often holistic, viewing the ocean as a complex, interconnected system that must be respected and maintained for future generations.

For example, indigenous knowledge systems have long recognized the importance of preserving fish breeding grounds, adjusting fishing practices in response to seasonal variations, and protecting critical marine habitats like mangroves and coral reefs. These practices are deeply rooted in the understanding that the health of the marine environment directly affects human well-being.

Role of Modern Innovations

Modern innovations in technology, data analytics, and scientific research have the potential to complement and amplify traditional practices. Satellite monitoring, GIS mapping, and marine sensors provide real-time data on ocean conditions, fish stock health, and pollution levels, enabling more precise and effective management strategies. Similarly, innovations in marine biotechnology, renewable energy, and sustainable aquaculture practices can address contemporary challenges such as overfishing, climate change, and resource depletion.

The use of digital tools and AI-powered systems for predictive modeling, environmental monitoring, and fisheries management can support and enhance the effectiveness of traditional resource management techniques. These technologies provide detailed, large-scale insights that can inform decision-making and improve the accuracy of traditional practices.

Synergies Between Traditional Knowledge and Modern Innovations

Integrating traditional knowledge with modern innovations creates a more comprehensive and adaptive approach to managing marine resources. Collaborative initiatives that combine the strengths of both can lead to solutions that are culturally relevant, scientifically robust, and context-specific. In fisheries management, for example, combining traditional catch limits with modern monitoring technologies can enhance sustainability while respecting cultural practices.

This integration not only strengthens the management of marine ecosystems but also empowers local communities by recognizing their knowledge and involving them in decision-making processes. It fosters a sense of ownership and responsibility, essential for the long-term success of the Blue Economy.

A Vision for the Blue Economy as a Pillar of Global Sustainability

The Blue Economy holds immense potential to be a cornerstone of global sustainability, driving economic growth while safeguarding the health of marine ecosystems. By harnessing ocean-based resources responsibly and equitably, the Blue Economy can contribute significantly to the achievement of the United Nations SDGs, particularly SDG 14 (Life Below Water), SDG 13 (Climate Action), and SDG 8 (Decent Work and Economic Growth). This vision requires a holistic approach that integrates environmental conservation, economic development, and social equity, ensuring that marine resources are used sustainably for the benefit of present and future generations.

Economic Growth through Sustainable Use of Ocean Resources

A sustainable Blue Economy embraces the idea that economic growth and environmental protection can coexist. By fostering industries such as sustainable fisheries, aquaculture, marine renewable energy, and eco-tourism, the Blue Economy can generate significant wealth while minimizing ecological degradation. Innovative technologies, such as AI-driven fisheries management, offshore renewable energy installations, and sustainable aquaculture systems, can ensure that these industries contribute to long-term economic prosperity without exhausting marine resources.

The transition to a Blue Economy requires a shift from short-term exploitation to long-term sustainability. By prioritizing investments in sustainable industries and circular economy practices—such as reducing waste, recycling marine products, and promoting eco-friendly designs—nations can create resilient economies that are less vulnerable to the risks posed by environmental degradation and climate change.

Environmental Stewardship and Ecosystem Restoration

Central to the vision of a Blue Economy is the recognition that healthy marine ecosystems are vital to human well-being and economic success. As such, the Blue Economy must prioritize ecosystem restoration and conservation. Protecting critical habitats like coral reefs, mangroves, and seagrass beds is essential for biodiversity, carbon sequestration, and coastal protection.

MPAs and integrated coastal zone management strategies are key tools for maintaining the health of marine ecosystems. By setting aside significant portions of marine areas for conservation and enhancing the resilience of these ecosystems to climate change, the Blue Economy can ensure that the oceans continue to provide essential services, such as food security, climate regulation, and water purification.

Social Equity and Inclusive Development

A sustainable Blue Economy also promotes social equity by ensuring that coastal and island communities—often the most dependent on marine resources—benefit from ocean-based industries. This includes creating equitable access to sustainable livelihoods, empowering women and marginalized groups, and fostering community-driven resource management. Integrating traditional knowledge with modern scientific practices can further strengthen the inclusivity of ocean governance.

Ultimately, the Blue Economy must serve as a vehicle for both environmental sustainability and social justice, ensuring that its growth is inclusive, resilient, and aligned with global sustainability objectives.

Future Directions for Research and Practice

As the Blue Economy continues to evolve, future research and practice must address emerging challenges and capitalize on new opportunities to ensure its sustainability. Interdisciplinary approaches that combine marine science, economics, technology, and social sciences are essential for developing comprehensive solutions to complex ocean-related issues.

One key area for future research is improving the understanding of marine ecosystems and their responses to climate change. As ocean acidification, warming temperatures, and shifting ecosystems affect marine biodiversity, there is an urgent need for more advanced research on ecosystem resilience and adaptation. This knowledge is crucial for effective conservation strategies and sustainable resource management.

Technological innovation will also play a pivotal role in shaping the future of the Blue Economy. Research into advanced monitoring tools, such as remote sensing technologies, AI-powered predictive models, and blockchain for traceability in supply chains, can enhance decision-making and improve the sustainability of ocean industries. Additionally, the development of renewable energy solutions, such as floating wind farms and tidal energy systems, offers significant potential for reducing carbon emissions and transitioning to cleaner energy sources.

Another important direction for research is understanding the socio-economic impacts of Blue Economy activities. Future studies should focus on how ocean industries affect local communities, particularly in terms of employment, income, and social equity. Exploring how to ensure that the benefits of the Blue Economy are shared equitably, especially in coastal and island communities, is crucial for fostering inclusive development.

Lastly, integrating traditional knowledge with modern innovations remains a key area for advancing Blue Economy practices. Research that bridges indigenous ecological knowledge with contemporary scientific methods can enhance the sustainability and effectiveness of marine resource management. Moving forward, this integration will be vital for creating resilient and adaptive systems in the Blue Economy.

www.ingramcontent.com/pod-product-compliance
Lightning Source LLC
Chambersburg PA
CBHW052139270326
41930CB00012B/2944